APPLEBY HOUSE

'In theory, this short book should be about as interesting as a shopping list . . . It is, however, packed with little pen-portraits of the residents, their dodgy hot water systems, their boyfriends, washing lines, toilet rolls, home-knitted jumpers, and their landlords – a surprisingly readable and sweet celebration of ordinary stuff happening to ordinary people'
Big Issue

'Smith's chronicle of ordinary life, its exhausting trivialities, relationships and annoyances, is written in sparsely simple but engaging prose'
Nottingham Evening Post

'Riveting . . . Her style is engagingly simple and, combined with unsparing honesty and an overwhelming interest in her subject, makes for a delightful little tale of London life'
Metro London

Born in East London to working-class parents as the Second World War was drawing to its close, Sylvia Smith ducked out of a career in hairdressing at the last minute to begin a life of office work. She slowly and completely accidentally worked her way up to the position of private secretary. She is unmarried with no children. A driving licence and a school swimming certificate are her only qualifications, although she is also quite good at dressmaking. *Misadventures* was published by Canongate in 2001. *Appleby House* is her second book.

also by Sylvia Smith

MISADVENTURES

APPLEBY HOUSE

Sylvia Smith

PICADOR

First published 2002 by Picador

This edition published 2003 by Picador
an imprint of Pan Macmillan Ltd
Pan Macmillan, 20 New Wharf Road, London N1 9RR
Basingstoke and Oxford
Associated companies throughout the world
www.panmacmillan.com

ISBN 0 330 49128 8

1 3 5 7 9 8 6 4 2

A CIP catalogue record for this book is available from
the British Library.

Typeset by Intype London Ltd
Printed and bound in Great Britain by
Mackays of Chatham plc, Chatham, Kent

I dedicate this book to all the other tenants
with whom I shared furnished accommodation over
the years for all the good times and even the bad.

The words in this book tell the true story of one year
of my life spent in a furnished house in east London.
I have changed the names of the other tenants to save
possible embarrassment, but I have not changed the
names of the landlords, Mr and Mrs Appleby – a
nicer couple you could not meet.

Sylvia Smith

APPLEBY HOUSE

Appleby House 2002
sporting a new roof, new windows, new garden wall
and a coat of paint. It has been converted into two
flats. There is still no gate.

East London, August 1984

Aged thirty-eight years I rang the bell of Appleby House one Wednesday evening in late August, early for my appointment with Mr and Mrs Appleby. They were the landlords of the property, advertising a bedsit with a separate kitchen to rent through a local accommodation agency. A plump, dark-haired girl answered the door, wearing a shorty dressing gown.

I said, 'I'm due to see Mr and Mrs Appleby at eight. I realize I'm early, but are they here yet?'

'I'm afraid not, but they're usually prompt.' she replied, adding as she slowly closed the door, 'I shouldn't think they'll be too long.'

As I wasn't invited in I returned to my brown Renault 5 car parked opposite the house, hoping the Applebys wouldn't be late.

I looked at the house. It didn't look very encouraging from the outside. It was terraced with peeling paintwork and the shabbiest in the street. There were bricks missing from the low brick wall and no gate to the unevenly paved path. Two rusty dustbins were squeezed into the small front garden and a lone rose bush struggled for survival amongst the weeds.

Five minutes early, a white station wagon parked outside the house. An elderly couple alighted and walked up to the street door. I went over to them and asked, 'Are you Mr and Mrs Appleby?'

'Yes, that's right, dear,' was the friendly reply from Mrs Appleby. Mr Appleby gave me a warm smile.

I said, 'I'm Sylvia Smith and I've come to see you about the room.'

Mr Appleby opened the street door and we entered the house. I looked around me. There was no carpet in the hallway but brown lino, which also covered the stairs and what I could see of the upstairs landing. There was an old-fashioned dresser with a mirror ahead of me and a small public telephone box on the wall beside it, with a slot for 10p coins. The hall was to the right of the house. The first door we came to on the left had a small steel plate screwed onto it in the shape of the figure '1'. The door immediately next to this was unnumbered.

Mr Appleby told me, 'This is Flat 1 and the door next to it is its kitchen. At the far end of the hall you can see another door with "2" on it. That's Flat 2, which has a kitchen added onto it at the back. The door on the right of Flat 2 leads down to the cellar.'

The Applebys and I proceeded up the linoed stairs into a linoed hallway. They took me to the back of the house and showed me the kitchen that would be mine, overlooking the back garden. It was partitioned from another kitchen which they explained belonged to Flat 4. The partition equally divided the one window.

My kitchen was cream in colour, very compact, and the gas cooker looked brand new. There was a meter beside the cooker which took 50p coins.

We walked to the front of the house, passing the bathroom and separate toilet and up the three stairs to the room marked '3'. Mr Appleby unlocked the door and ushered me in.

It was a pleasant room in the middle of the house, with a window from which you could see the side of the house next door, its yard and back garden. To the right you could see the side of 'our' house, our pathway and the dividing high brown wooden fence and the left side of our back garden. I looked around the room. There was a single bed against the far wall and everything was shabbily furnished in either red or white, with the walls, wardrobe, wall cupboard, bedside chest of drawers and fridge in white and two armchairs, the carpet and curtains in red. Mr Appleby switched on the brown electric fire with its revolving red light, which gave the impression of a fire glowing through its plastic coals.

I warmed immediately to Mr and Mrs Appleby, whom I felt were a nice couple. Mrs Appleby was a slim blonde woman of sixty-five years, with a kindly smile. Her husband was thickset with dark hair and was very tall. He looked much younger than her, but I was later to find he simply looked younger than his years and was of a similar age. Mrs Appleby and I sat down in the armchairs and, as there was nowhere else to sit, Mr Appleby sat on the bed.

We discussed the accommodation, the rules of the house and the rent, which was payable weekly.

Mrs Appleby explained, 'Although the accommodation is for only one person, we do allow everyone to have boyfriends at weekends if they want. Also all the tenants in this house have been very carefully selected and they're all young English women.'

I interrupted. 'Is my age going to be a problem here?'

Mrs Appleby replied, 'No, I don't think so, dear. The young woman next door is in her early thirties and she gets on very well here.' Mrs Appleby continued, warmly describing her tenants, telling me, 'I have a lovely little girl in the front room downstairs and a very professional young woman next door to you.

'The young girl in Number 2 is moving out shortly into her own flat. Also, the girl in Number 4 has lived here for several years, so despite the fact that her room is much larger than yours we have kept her rent much lower as we consider her a valued tenant. The little girl downstairs is an art student without much money so we only charge her £25 a week for her two rooms, although we realize we could get considerably more than that if we wanted to.'

Mr Appleby added, 'You should find this a very friendly house.'

I asked Mrs Appleby, 'Did you ever live here?'

'Yes, dear,' she replied. 'My parents bought the house when they married. I was born here and lived here until I married. When my parents died they left it to me as I was an only child, and I've let it out ever since.'

As we got on so well, it was decided I would move in the following Saturday. I supplied the necessary references and signed a six months' lease, paying a deposit of £100 and two weeks' rent in advance at the rate of £23 per week.

We returned to the hall. Mr Appleby showed me the door marked 4, where 'the professional young woman' lived, and the two electricity meters on the wall opposite my room, which took 10p coins, one of which was mine. Both meters were above an armchair piled high with newspapers and magazines.

Mr Appleby said, 'Don't worry about running out of coins, you can always get them off us on a Sunday when we collect the rents as we empty the meters at the same time.'

I said goodbye to the Applebys and left the house with my copy of the lease and my keys, and looked forward to moving in on the Saturday.

On the Saturday afternoon I drove to Appleby House, my small car packed to the brim with my belongings. It was market day in the local High Street, and as the house was in one of the side turnings, there were no parking spaces available outside it. I drove around the block and was forced to park at the bottom of the road. I walked up the street with my shopping bag full of groceries, keys in hand, fully expecting several long tramps bringing my possessions into my room. To my delight a young couple returned to their car parked outside the house and were obviously about to drive away. I asked the young man, 'Could you wait two minutes before you go because I'm moving into this house today and I'd like to park outside instead of down the street where I am at the moment?'

'All right, love,' he replied and duly waited for me to fetch my car.

The laborious job of moving in began. I made countless trips from my car to the house, lugging dustbin bags up the stairs all bursting with clothing, bedding, bath towels, kitchenware, and lastly my white suitcase packed tight with dresses. I piled the lot into the middle of my room, thoroughly exhausted, and thought, 'Thank God that's over.' I took teabags, milk and sweeteners from my shopping bag and made myself a refreshing cup of tea.

There was total silence in the house. I leaned over the banisters and called out, 'Is anyone in?' There was no reply. I returned to my room and looked at the huge mound of possessions piled in the middle of it. It was nightfall before I had found a place for everything.

A few days later I looked through the post on the

hall dresser and opened an envelope addressed to me. It was an invoice from the accommodation agency claiming a week and a half's rent in payment of their introduction fee to the house.

The House and Its Occupants

The first person to return to the house was the 'very professional young woman' who lived in the room next door to mine.

She slammed the street door behind her and clattered up the stairs. When I heard her footsteps approaching my door I opened mine and saw a tall, slim and attractive brunette.

'Hello,' I said. 'I'm Sylvia the new tenant.'

She smiled at me and said, 'I'm Laura,' and, looking over my shoulder at my pile of belongings, added, 'looks like you're going to have a good time there.' She unlocked her door and entered her room, banging the door shut.

During the course of the day I heard the street door opening and closing and gathered everybody was in. Whilst cleaning my kitchen I soon found the top of the stairs to be a good meeting place as people paid visits to the bathroom and loo.

The second person to climb the stairs was Sharon, the plump, dark-haired girl I had met on the evening of my interview with the Applebys. She was quite pretty. She walked towards me with a big smile on her face and greeted me with a cheery 'Hi.' We were soon deep in conversation.

'I see you're busy cleaning your kitchen,' she said. 'I cleaned your room for you.'

'That was very nice of you,' I replied. 'How bad was it?'

'It was bloody filthy,' was the reply. 'The last girl in there wasn't very clean at all. There were dirty knickers in the wardrobe and everywhere was very mucky.

'What do you do for a living?' she asked.

'I'm a secretary to a managing director of a gents' clothing firm,' I replied. 'It's easy to get to. I've got a car and it takes about twenty minutes to drive there, and he's a very nice boss. What do you do?'

'Well, I'm only nineteen,' she replied, 'and I'm an art student at college. When I've qualified I hope to start my own business in interior design. My parents are quite well off and have a lot of contacts so that should be a good option.'

'Why don't you live at home?' I asked.

'Well, my parents are based in the Middle East as my father's an engineer out there. They've got a flat in west London, but I live here with my boyfriend Peter and if I lived in my parents' flat they'd find out about Peter and I don't think they'd be too pleased about it. Oh.' She paused. 'Don't tell the Applebys that Peter lives here, we're not supposed to double up, you know.'

'All right, I won't say a word,' I assured her. 'Have you lived in the Middle East?' I queried.

'Yes,' she replied. 'My parents took me there with my older sister when I was about three, but things got a bit nasty, so when I was seven they sent both of us to boarding school over here to keep us out of danger. My sister's married these days and lives in this country in Surrey with her husband. My parents come over here about twice a year and they know I go out with Peter, but they don't know I live with him. By the way,' she added, 'the girl who had your room used to share it with her fiancé, but the Applebys don't know that one either.'

Laura walked down the hallway. Sharon said, 'Hi,' as Laura entered her kitchen. Sharon raised her eyes, indicating that she didn't think too much of Laura. She said, 'I'll see you later,' and disappeared into the loo.

I continued cleaning my kitchen and began chatting to Laura, who I could clearly hear pottering about in hers through our thin partition.

'How long have you been here?' I asked.

'Four years,' was the reply.

'What are you doing in there?' I queried as I could hear a loud hissing sound.

'I'm cooking with a wok. I always have a proper cooked meal every evening.'

There was a silence, then she asked, 'How old are you?'

'Thirty-eight,' I replied.

'Blimey,' she said. 'You're lucky they let you in.'

'How old are you?' I asked.

'Thirty-one,' was the reply.

I didn't think our age gap was too vast.

Ignoring her comment, I continued, 'How do we get on with the washing here?'

She replied, 'There's a launderette about a hundred yards down the main road. You turn right out of here, then do another right at the corner and it's halfway down on the left. It's very good and we all use it, but I think the others usually dry their things in the drier. I prefer to hang my stuff in the back garden. You have to go through someone's kitchen downstairs to get out there. Sharon usually lets me through hers.' She paused and said, 'I like to do my washing on a Sunday.'

'So do I,' I replied.

'Can't you do yours on a Saturday instead?' she snapped.

I looked through my half of the window at the back garden below and replied, 'Well, there's two long washing lines out there. You tell me which one you want and I'll take the other. I can't do my washing on Saturdays. I'm too busy shopping and cooking.'

'All right, I'll have the one on the path,' was the irritated reply.

Our discussion ended at this point. There was much hissing and clanging of pans. Laura eventually emerged from her kitchen with a mysterious green concoction on a tray, which she took to her room.

I spent my time going back and forth from my room to my kitchen. Whilst cooking my dinner I heard footsteps coming up the stairs. This time it was Susanna from Flat 2. It was now early evening. She was wearing a short nightshirt with her long slim legs on display, carrying a bath towel and a toilet bag.

She looked about twenty-two and had short mousy hair. She smiled and said, 'Hello,' as she went into the bathroom. On her way back she stopped to talk. She introduced me to a teenage blonde who was closing the street door behind her.

'This is Beverley, my kid sister,' she said. Beverley smiled at me from the bottom of the stairs. Susanna continued, 'She's only fourteen and she's staying with me as our parents are in Germany. My father's a British soldier and he's just been posted there. Our parents have bought a two-bedroomed flat over here which me and Beverley will be moving into once everything goes through. Don't tell the Applebys that Beverley's here,' she said. 'She isn't supposed to be. Well, I hope you like it here,' she said as she went down the stairs.

The toilet was an absolute disgrace. When I voiced this complaint to Sharon, she replied, 'Well, I do give it a swipe occasionally, but I don't think anyone else bothers.' On looking at the toilet I agreed she only gave it a swipe. The seat appeared to be clean, but, looking down the pan, it was quite clear no one had 'bothered' with it for some considerable time. As I got to know Laura, I discovered she usually emptied her teapot down it and also any leftover gravy. The entire closet was covered in dust and grime and it seemed to me that no one had cleaned it for about a year.

Also the toilet was rather old. On pulling the chain, not only did the sound of rushing water echo all over the house, but I was convinced the noise was so loud you could hear it three gardens up. Added to this, the sudden fierce rush of water would hit the bottom of the loo and spit over the occupant. I soon discovered the way to miss this was to pull the chain and jump back quickly.

As I was only a tenant I could do no more than to suggest to the others that we have a weekly rota for cleaning the toilet. Although everyone agreed to this, no one ever came forward to do so. The next time I went shopping I bought disposable plastic gloves, a huge bottle of bleach, disinfectant and a scrubbing brush and spent one hour thoroughly sterilizing the entire toilet. I did mention the subject of cleaning again, but no one ever bothered, so cleaning the loo became part of my Saturday routine throughout my stay in Appleby House.

I decided I would like to have a bath and wash my now lank brown hair, and inspected the bathroom. It contained an old white bath and washbasin, with a large frosted window covered by a blue blind with blue lino on the floor. Over the bath there were several wooden bars hanging from the ceiling for the drying of washing.

I looked at the old heater and slot meter beside it. Unable to see clearly what to do, I went downstairs and knocked on Sharon's door for assistance. She followed me up the stairs and explained, 'This is the heater and the slot meter, it takes 50p coins. In the summer the water heats up quicker and you always get two full baths for your 50p. The only snag is that when you put your 50p in one day and go to have another bath the next day, you usually find someone has nicked your water. It's all right for me and Peter. I usually have the first bath and then, when I can persuade him to have a bath, he follows me. That way we get full value for our 50p.' She added, 'It's one hell of a job to get Peter in the bath, you know. He just doesn't like washing too much.' She continued, 'In the winter the water takes much longer to heat up and then you usually only get two half baths.'

She held out her hand and said, 'Give me your 50p, and I'll start this bath for you.' I gave it to her and she soon had hot water gushing out of the tap.

'Thanks, Sharon,' I said.

She said, 'By the way, we take it in turns to put out toilet rolls in the loo. Everyone has a different colour. You'll follow green, so when that runs out you replace it with your colour, which is orange. Just stick it in the holder and wait until green turns up again, then after that you supply an orange one.'

'Ok, Sharon,' I said, 'Thanks very much. Bye,' as she disappeared down the stairs.

As I slowly met the other tenants, I saw their accommodation. Laura had the upstairs front room, which was the largest room in the house. From the door you could see a long stereo unit on the left-hand wall, followed by shelving filled with books. The far wall had two large windows overlooking the street, with long net curtains and pale blue over curtains. Along the right-hand wall there was a single bed. In the middle of the room there was a very worn and old-fashioned blue two-seater settee with a matching armchair, and a large coloured TV was placed in front of the settee. A mottled brown carpet covered the floor. One day Laura surprised me by saying, 'I just can't keep up with the housework.' Also she would pile read newspapers and magazines on the armchair outside our rooms.

Laura was the only tenant who genuinely lived on her own and had never had anyone share her accommodation. Although she knew all the others doubled up and only paid the one rent, never at any time did she tell the Applebys. From conversations

I had with her whilst in our kitchens, I discovered she had a good job as a computer operator in the City and was very well paid. Unfortunately Laura was not the quietest of people. She loved loud music and a loud TV.

Sharon quite rightly said, 'I think I've got the best accommodation in the house.' She had the large front room downstairs and the large kitchen next to it with French windows leading to the back garden. As you opened the door to her front room, you faced a large single bed against the wall which she shared with Peter.

'How do you both get in there?' I queried.

'Peter sleeps on the outside and I'm the one who's usually squeezed up against the wall,' she explained.

The bed was in the recess on the right of the fireplace. In the left recess there was high white shelving which she used as a bookcase. There was a grey carpet on the floor and soft cream over curtains and half nets in the large bay window. A small white chest of drawers was squashed against the hearth, the entire top of which was covered in miniature bottles all filled with perfume. The chest looked out of place as it protruded into the middle of the room. There was a pale yellow armchair beside the chest and several dolls were hanging by strings from the ceiling. A dozen soft toys were scattered around the room. On the left wall behind the door there was a large white chest of drawers and a mahogany double wardrobe.

Sharon proudly told me, 'I've done the Applebys a favour by stripping and revarnishing this wardrobe.' I looked at the wardrobe. It seemed very streaky to me.

Sharon's kitchen was an absolute eyesore. Peter's motorbike outfit and crash helmet were leaning against the left wall. Beside them were various artwork canvases and paint brushes on the dark orange lino, and a small white fridge. The table in the middle of the room was piled high with kitchen equipment. Clothing was folded over the two chairs. Against the back wall were French windows, an old electric cooker, and a large sink unit covered with clean pots and pans.

Peter fitted very well into the house. He was a young man of twenty-three and our only male occupant. He had a motorbike which he housed in the tiny front garden. He worked as a despatch rider delivering parcels and messages in the City on his motorbike. He was tall, slim and dark, and Sharon and he were very wrapped up in each other.

*

Susanna's accommodation comprised a single bed along the right-hand wall facing the door. A shabby blue two-seater settee sat in the bay window. The window faced the high wooden fencing dividing our yard from next door. A colour TV was placed on top of a large chest of drawers against the left-hand wall. There was a large cupboard to the right of the door, which served as a wardrobe. At the far end of the room a glass door led surprisingly onto a very smart kitchen, which had a good table and two chairs in it, plus an almost new cooker, fridge and sink unit. The kitchen had a back door leading into the garden.

Susanna told me she worked as a copy typist for a local company and didn't earn very much money.

Susanna wasn't very pleased with Laura's loud stereo. She told me, 'One night the music was so loud Beverley wasn't able to concentrate on her schoolwork, so I went to see Laura and asked her to turn it down a bit. She only refused! It wasn't as if I'd asked her to turn it off. I just said, "Could you turn it down, please," and she told me, "No." So I said, "You're a mean cow, Laura." And I live at the back of the house miles away from her.'

'What happened after that?' I asked.

'Oh, well,' she replied, 'Laura left it blaring so

bang went Beverley's homework. Laura's the most selfish cow I've ever met.'

There was a large garden at the back of the house. It was very overgrown with knee-high grass and bushes at the end of it. A high dividing fence covered the back yard, with a much lower fence dividing the gardens.

Mr and Mrs Appleby

Mr and Mrs Appleby lived in their own property in a leafy suburb of London. Every Sunday around noon Mr Appleby would drive his wife to Appleby House to collect the rents and empty the meters. This was the only time they visited the house unless there were repairs to see to, when Mr Appleby would arrive by himself, usually during daytime, to put matters right.

They were both smartly but casually dressed, but I never saw Mrs Appleby wear anything other than trousers. Her hair was dyed blonde and she wore spectacles.

They were excellent landlords to all their tenants and were a very genuine and kindly couple.

It seemed to me that Mr Appleby was in charge of their relationship. He would order Mrs Appleby about, sometimes scolding her. Mrs Appleby would always do as her husband told her without complaint.

They were a childless couple and I wondered if they had married late in life.

Laura

Laura was a single woman who had never married. She was always beautifully dressed and had an enormous supply of clothing.

She took great care of herself, cooking a nourishing meal every evening and not smoking cigarettes. She attended aerobics and weight-lifting sessions at the local sports centre and had all the appropriate clothing: leotard, leggings and trainers with thick colourful sport socks.

Her father and brother regularly visited her on a

Sunday evening. She had one best girlfriend whom she went out with and spoke to on the telephone, but the girlfriend rarely came to the house.

She had a long-term man friend she would see every few weeks, but the relationship was strictly platonic and he did not stay overnight. Laura told me, 'It's just nice to have a man's company once in a while.' Sharon, being unkind, told me, 'In the two years I've lived here Laura has only had one man stay the night and that was only because he missed his last train and she had to put him up on the sofa.'

We all knew Laura had a high salary and we wondered why she did not buy herself her own flat, but she seemed content living in Appleby House.

Sharon

S haron's life revolved around art college and Peter. She had two days off college each week to study and would spend the time in her flat. She usually wore blue denims and a jumper or T-shirt. She was a very lively personality, full of conversation.

Sharon and Peter had a few friends who would occasionally spend an evening with them in their flat, with Sharon cooking the dinner, but they rarely went out together at night.

Sharon would phone her parents in the Middle

East every few weeks, using the phone box in the hall, and would proudly boast that the calls only cost her 10p a time. This situation ended when the telephone engineer called and converted the phone to the updated pricing system. Soon after this a telephone bill arrived for the Applebys. Fearing there might be some reference to her almost free calls, Sharon decided the best thing to do was to find out. She steamed the envelope open, read its contents and, reassured, resealed it and left it on the hall dresser for the Applebys to collect. This event went unnoticed by the Applebys.

Sharon's parents frequently phoned her, but Sharon and her mother were not good friends and would often have flaming rows, with Sharon yelling and swearing down the telephone saying, 'I hate you, you f——— bitch.' Her voice would echo throughout the house. After these rows Sharon's sister usually phoned in an attempt to sort things out, but to no avail. Sharon did not like her mother at all and would tell me she was 'a drunken slob who can't keep off the bottle'.

Unfortunately for Sharon, her father paid a visit to London and discovered she and Peter were living together. He was very upset, but Sharon insisted the relationship would continue. He decided not to tell her mother.

Peter

Peter usually spent his evenings in the front room with Sharon. He did not involve himself with either me or Laura. Practically the only time I came into contact with him was entering and leaving the house, or when he went to the bathroom or loo. He would usually run up the stairs and if he saw Laura or me he would simply say 'Hello' as he dashed past. Laura rarely attempted to get into conversation with him. I did. He was always polite to me, but I got the impression he would leave me at his first opportunity.

He was well spoken but was not educated as Sharon was and he seemed quite content with just working as a messenger. He didn't appear to have many clothes. All I ever saw him in was his leather motorbike outfit or a pair of jeans and I noticed he possessed four jumpers and a couple of shirts.

Apart from his motorbike, his only interest seemed to be music. Once he spoke to me long enough to borrow my tape recorder for a few evenings to tape the latest tunes.

He was always in the house on a Sunday when the Applebys came to collect the rents, but neither he nor Sharon seemed worried that the Applebys might realize he lived there.

His mother would phone him at regular intervals, but none of his relations ever came to the house. He and Sharon would go to dinner at his parents' home occasionally. He had a lot of fun with Sharon. Apart from their rows, I would hear laughter from downstairs front.

I would describe him as 'a nice boy'.

The Neighbours

It was Laura who told me of Mo's circumstances. Mo was aged forty and lived in the house next door with her four children. She was English and had married a Turk when she was very young and had two children by him. The marriage broke up, her husband returned to Turkey, but they did not divorce. A few years later her husband returned to London, they re-kindled their marriage and Mo gave birth to a further two children. Once again her husband left her and returned to his country, but this time he stayed there.

Laura and Mo were very good friends. When Laura hung her washing in the back garden they would talk over the dividing fence. They would occasionally go out together, to bingo or to the cinema.

If Mo and I were in our back gardens we would chat to each other, but we did not become more than neighbourly.

I didn't know Mo's financial circumstances, but she and her family were well dressed. I would see full washing lines of spotlessly clean clothing and bed-linen in her back garden.

She owned a lovely old black mongrel called Bess. Bess would excrete daily in the yard. Mo would wash this onto the earth using a bucket of disinfected water and a yard broom.

The house on our right was owned by a young Pakistani couple. They had two little girls aged four and six, and they shared their home with the wife's mother.

Hanging my washing out on a Sunday, I would see the children playing in their garden. I always stopped to talk to them and, at their request, would search our high grass for the ball they had accidentally knocked over.

One Sunday I was talking to the children, who were leaning out of their upstairs bathroom window.

Hearing his children's voices and wondering where they were, the father came out into the back garden. He looked at me and at his bathroom. His curiosity satisfied, he silently went indoors without glancing at me further.

The Pakistani children were very noisy. They would shout and laugh as they played in the garden and would run around their house slamming doors and screeching. The old man who lived next door to them would lean over their back fence shouting at the family. 'You are making too much noise. You are upsetting my wife. You are making too much noise. You are upsetting my wife.' He would drone on and on, with the noise in the house still continuing. On one occasion I heard Mo yell from her kitchen, 'Oh shut up!' This did not deter him.

I did not come into contact with any other neighbours and, this being a typical London street, I would only have recognized a few.

Life in the House

Everything started off very well. There was no problem with Laura and the washing lines on a Sunday and I found her very pleasant.

Even the bath situation was easily sorted out, despite turning the tap on the following day to find someone had used my hot water. I talked to the others one by one and suggested, 'Why don't we all put our 50p pieces in the meter when we want a bath, remember we have one left, take it, then play fair, don't take someone else's and put another 50p in the meter. That way we should all have full value for our money.' Everyone agreed to this, solving the problem of the bath during the warm summer months.

On one of Sharon's trips up the stairs, she said to me, 'Sylvia, have you noticed the keyhole to the bathroom is plugged up with tissue paper?'

'No, is it?' I replied, taking a look at it.

'I think that's Laura in case Peter peeps through at her,' she said and disappeared into the loo with a cheeky grin on her face.

If Sharon's guess was correct, I had noticed another idiosyncrasy of Laura's. One evening I was very puzzled to see Laura take her transistor radio into the loo. When she switched it on quite loudly immediately after closing the door, I realized why she had done this.

During the few weeks I knew Susanna and Beverley, I found both girls very polite and friendly. They would spend time with Sharon and Peter, having the occasional night out together.

Sometimes of an evening I would hear yells and shouts coming from Sharon and Peter's front room. I discovered they took it in turns to pull and pinch various parts of each other's bodies. At other times they would have flaming rows, with Peter slamming out of the house late at night, leaving Sharon in tears, wondering if he was going to return.

The first time this happened a tearful Sharon told me her troubles.

I suggested, 'Would you like one of my sleeping tablets? My doctor said anyone can take them.' Adding, 'At least you'll get to sleep.'

'All right, I'll take one,' she replied.

Sharon and Peter were to have many more rows, each one resulting with Sharon taking a sleeping tablet and Peter returning halfway through the night.

Mr Appleby would come to the house for repair work. He would arrive mid-afternoon, minus a flask. When I came in of an evening I always offered him a cup of tea, which he would gratefully accept. Whilst carrying out these repairs he would happily sing at the top of his voice. 'Ramona, I hear the mission bells above. Ramona . . .'. I thoroughly enjoyed his off-key rendition, which echoed through the house.

He was also very much a father figure. He had young females floating past him in their shorty night-dresses, legs on display, but he never took the slightest bit of notice.

*

One evening I was alone in the house and rather nervous because of this. Hearing the street door open and close, I called over the banisters, 'Who is it?' to hear the reassuring voice of Mr Appleby. 'It's only me.'

When the telephone rang it was clearly heard all over the house and you could also hear everyone's conversation. Sharon found a way round this. If a call was private and she didn't want to be overheard, she would take the receiver into her room and push her door to, leaving the cord stretched from the box straight across the hall at neck level.

Laura almost shouted on the telephone, so the entire house noticed that she would sometimes hold a conversation in a foreign language.

'She's speaking Spanish,' Sharon would say. 'I do speak a bit,' she added, 'and her Spanish isn't very good. Most of the time she's saying numbers, so perhaps it's some special code and I think it's only to this particular girlfriend of hers.'

There was no type of housework rota to cover the communal facilities. Sharon would vacuum the downstairs hall, leaving Laura and me to vacuum the stairs and upper hallway. Laura always did this more times than I did. Never at any time during my twelve months' stay did anyone wash the stairs or hallways.

Laura would wash the bathroom floor every few weeks. Noticing a dirty bath and knowing it was Peter, she would shout over the banisters, 'You haven't cleaned this bath out again, have you?' Neither Sharon nor Peter would reply, but Sharon did usually clean the bath after Peter and I always found it clean.

Sharon was always very friendly towards me and would often chat to me while I cooked my evening meal. Whenever she saw Laura she would smile and say, 'Hi,' but when Laura was out of earshot she would talk about her, saying, 'I'm always very careful to keep on the right side of Laura. I know how nasty she can be. How are you getting on with her and her music?'

'Well,' I replied, 'I must admit it's a bit on the loud side sometimes, but I always find her very friendly and pleasant.'

Sharon continued, 'Everybody who has ever had your room has always complained about Laura's music. The couple before you had a terrible time. They were always asking her to turn it down, but she never would. They were always rowing. We're not too bad downstairs, but on occasions the vibration of the drumbeats have been so loud our light goes up and down from the ceiling. But I think

Peter and I have been very good, we've only complained to her once and just asked her to turn a speaker down as the beat was so loud. And she did. Apart from that, I don't like her very much at all. She's always got something nasty to say.'

As the days passed by I noticed Laura's stereo and TV were slowly getting louder. Eventually her noise filled my room and I had difficulty hearing my radio. I was reluctant to complain, but I intended buying myself a TV set and realized I would be unable to hear it. I knocked on her door.

I said, 'I'm sorry, Laura, but can you turn down the volume because I can't hear a thing in my room.'

She replied, 'All right, all right, I will. I don't want any trouble.'

She turned down the sound so low I could no longer hear it. This really pleased me and I thought how unpopular she was with the other tenants and I decided this was unjust.

The three girls downstairs would stop and chat when they saw me, but they would not say more than 'Hi' to Laura. Peter did say 'Hello' to both of us, but he would never stop to talk.

I felt very sorry for Laura, being so isolated. I always tried to bring her into any conversation with the others and I did my best to make friends with her. This situation continued for a few weeks, then sud-

denly my life changed. Up went Laura's stereo and
TV until my room was full of her noise.

Once again I knocked on her door to complain,
but this time she said, 'I think I'm entitled to play
my music loud after a hard day's work,' and shut the
door in my face, leaving the noise to continue.

I complained frequently, but usually she ignored
my requests.

One night unable to sleep at eleven-thirty I
knocked on her door, asking, 'Can you turn down
your TV please, Laura?

She called out, 'It's down.'

As it was I went back to bed and eventually fell
asleep.

Living next door to Laura made life unpleasant
and I considered what I could do about it.

On one occasion Laura amused me but infuriated
the others. I could not believe my ears when I heard
her washing up at eleven-fifteen one week night. She
followed this by vacuuming her room. I considered
this to be so thoughtless it was funny, but the following day I heard the complaints from downstairs.

It was some weeks before I noticed we had a
problem with the toilet rolls. Although we each had
our own colour, it was not always possible to buy
this, with the result that someone would just grab
whatever colour they could find and put this in the

holder. This resulted in pink being put out instead of blue and total confusion as to whose turn it was for the next roll. Laura was the only tenant in the house who knew exactly whose turn it was and seeing the empty holder would knock on that person's door, rudely saying, 'It's your turn to put out the toilet roll, you know!'

The Arrival of Tracey

Susanna and Beverley moved into their parents' flat at the end of October. The terms of our lease stated that the accommodation had to be in a clean condition on a tenant's departure. The girls spent considerable time thoroughly springcleaning the two rooms. They returned to the house at regular intervals to see Sharon and Peter.

Life in the house continued with Laura's loud TV and stereo, and with Sharon and Peter going through a good patch.

Flat 2 remained vacant for two weeks. Its next occupant was Tracey, a blonde twenty-four-year-old. I didn't see her at her interview with the Applebys, but I saw her move in on the Friday evening, with a middle-aged man helping her carry her few suitcases, stereo and two speakers.

My first meeting with Tracey was whilst I was cooking my dinner. She climbed the stairs and introduced herself, saying, 'Hello, I'm Tracey from downstairs,' in a soft shy voice. Enormous blue eyes looked at me and my first impression was what a sweet creature. We were soon deep in conversation.

I asked her, 'Who moved you in?'

'That was my uncle,' she replied.

'That was very nice of him,'

'Not really,' she replied. 'He charged me petrol money.'

'Where have you moved from?' I asked.

'I'm separated from my husband,' she replied. 'I moved out of our house in Brentwood a few weeks ago and went to live with my gran in her studio flat in Dagenham, and now here I am.' She shrugged.

'Have you got any children?' I asked.

'No,' she replied.

'You didn't have much luggage with you,' I continued.

'No,' she said. 'I had this big clear out. I left my husband practically all the furniture and all I've got with me are a few clothes, the stereo, bedding and some bath towels. I'm going to get myself a new wardrobe.'

She paused and asked, 'What do you do for a living?'

'I'm a shorthand secretary,' I replied. 'What do you do?' I asked.

'I'm a sort of Girl Friday in the City,' she replied. 'How long have you lived here?'

'About twelve weeks,' I replied. 'I'll show you the bathroom,' I said, leading her there and explaining our system. I also showed her the toilet, saying, 'When you pull the chain, jump back quick otherwise you're going to get wet.'

Tracey settled into the house and became good friends with Sharon and Peter. The two girls soon had an arrangement where they took it in turns to shop and cook dinner for the three of them, using Sharon's kitchen.

Sharon was always telling me what a good cook she was and the complicated meal she was about to produce – lasagne or pizza. I quite believed her until she cooked chips. Smoke would fill her kitchen and waft all over the house. At these times I would open my kitchen window wide and shut the door of my bedsit.

Tracey eventually met Laura and simply said, 'Hi,' I presumed because Sharon had forewarned her. Tracey never involved herself with Laura and behind her back would say, 'That bloody music of hers. We should stick a note on her door saying, "Entrance to disco 50p." '

Tracey and I became good friends. As she woke up at seven a.m. for work and I had difficulty waking at a quarter to eight, she would climb the stairs every weekday and give me a call.

One morning she said, 'Sylvia, can I borrow your iron?' This meant I had to open my door. When I saw her in the evening she said, 'You should have seen yourself. You opened the door, pointed to your cupboard and then went straight back to bed.'

Life continued with Laura's loud music, her habit of slamming the street door, her heavy tread on the stairs and upper hallway, and her loud voice on the telephone.

My Life at the House

I returned home from the office at approximately five-thirty each evening and would cook myself a dinner that was easy to prepare, choosing something that I could place in the oven and take out one hour later. One dinner I chose was pork chop and jacket potatoes, and I would add a side salad. During the cooking time I would make myself a cup of tea and would usually be in time to see the early evening news on TV. After this I would have a bath. As soon as I was dressed my dinner would be ready to eat.

Occasionally I had a takeaway, there being a choice of four in the locality, but I would not eat chips as I usually watched my weight. If I was hungry after my dinner I would eat fruit.

I was organized as far as I could be, living in a room with a small makeshift kitchen. I was a smoker and kept a supply of cigarettes in the top drawer of my bedside chest. I considered it necessary to have sleeping tablets, painkillers, vitamins and plasters, which I stored at the foot of my wardrobe. I always had a bottle of wine in the fridge and a variety of fruit in my fruit bowl.

Every Saturday I bought the week's groceries, using a shopping trolley to carry the load. I housed the trolley in a corner of my kitchen.

As my parents were separated, I would visit my father every other Sunday for a few hours as he lived alone. I would see my mother the last Saturday of each month. My father lived in the family house. My mother shared a flat with her sister in Basildon. My mother and my aunt would travel to London by bus to spend the day with me. I would cook an excellent lunch and would provide a bottle of wine. They in turn would bring some useful present to recompense me. As I didn't possess a table, we would sit on cushions placed on the carpet and eat from my coffee table, half watching TV and chatting. We always finished the wine, with the result that we would become rather tiddly. We would enjoy our time together and at six-thirty they would leave to catch the bus home.

I had two girlfriends I would see every few weeks. One was called Jessica, a mousy-haired divorcee two years my senior. We would meet at noon on a Sunday and usually took the tube to Queensway, where we would have lunch, stroll around the shops, finally walking through Hyde Park to Speakers' Corner, and stopping for a coffee before making our way home.

My other girlfriend was Brenda, a brunette aged thirty-four, Jewish and married with two young children. We would spend an evening in a pub chatting, Brenda telling me, 'It makes a break from having the children all day.'

I had two men friends, but these were strictly platonic relationships.

I also belonged to two large social clubs and would travel to events in the east London area in my car.

On the evenings I was home, I would spend my time watching TV and knitting sweaters.

I became very friendly with Mrs Appleby. She would occasionally have a quick cup of tea with me on a

Sunday while her husband emptied the meters. During one visit she told me, 'A previous tenant of your room was a student nurse and she told us she wouldn't be able to pay her rent for a few weeks because she had to buy some expensive books for her studies, so we had to wait. And not content with that one, dear, she had a fire in her kitchen! My husband had to repaint it! Soon after this she left and told us to keep her deposit.'

My TV Set

As I did not possess a TV set I decided to buy a second-hand coloured one. I went to a local shop one Saturday and bought a reconditioned model with an aerial for the sum of £52. It had a three-month guarantee and I considered myself lucky the shop was able to deliver it later the same day.

When I returned to the house I told Sharon of my purchase. She came out of her kitchen to see it when the engineer delivered it.

For the first three days my TV worked perfectly,

but on the fourth day it developed a high-pitched hum which completely distorted the sound. As I was home early from work I went downstairs and phoned the shop to complain. They replied, 'We'll come round and replace it for you, but that set was one of our better models and I'm surprised it's playing up.'

I asked, 'What time can you come round with the next one, then, because I don't get in until about five-thirty?'

He replied, 'We close at five.'

'Hang on a minute,' I said.

I turned round and knocked on Sharon's door. Sharon popped her head out. 'Could you be in for the TV engineer?' I asked her.

'All right,' she replied, 'but I'm not in until about four-thirty.'

I asked, 'If I give you my keys, could you let the engineer in at a quarter to five for me?'

Sharon said, 'Yes, all right.'

I returned to the phone and agreed that the engineer would arrive at that time the following day.

The next evening I arrived home from work and knocked on the street door, which was opened by Sharon. She said, 'I let your TV man in, Sylvia, and he's given you another set. I stayed with him all the time, so everything's there. Here's your keys,' she said, handing them to me. I closed the street door, saying, 'Thanks very much, Sharon. I owe you a favour,' and went up the stairs to my room to see my 'new' TV.

On looking at the set I could see it was quite old, but I found it worked all right, at least to start with. A few days later the picture started slipping and I was unable to correct this. Once again I phoned the shop, this time from the office, and a fresh appointment was made for four forty-five the following day, with Sharon taking my keys and letting the engineer in to repair my TV.

The next evening I knocked on the street door, which was opened by Sharon.

'Did the engineer turn up?' I asked her.

'Yes,' she replied. 'I let him in again and I stayed with him all the time.'

'OK, thank you very much,' I said, taking my keys from her, and climbed the stairs to try out my repaired TV set.

The picture held for another few days, but then started slipping again. Once more I complained to the shop and was told, 'This time we'll replace your set with the very best TV in the shop, but you'll have to wait until twelve o'clock Saturday for it to be delivered.'

By now Sharon and I decided this was a huge joke

and I began to think I should have bought a brand-new TV.

Saturday arrived. Around noon the engineer knocked on the street door. I opened it at the same time as Sharon wiggled down the stairs in her shorty night gown, having just had a bath. The engineer stood motionless in the doorway clutching my next TV. His eyes examined every inch of Sharon until she disappeared into her front room. He then followed me along the hallway and up the stairs, carrying the TV set with him.

This time I had a lovely TV. I totally believed it was the best one in the shop and must have sold at a much higher price than my original one. My 'new' TV did not develop any faults and it lasted me throughout my stay at Appleby House.

Laura and Me

At this particular time Laura and I simply did not get on. She always had her stereo or TV far too loud. One Saturday morning I was shocked into waking. I found myself sitting up in bed thinking, 'What's going on?', only to find Laura had her stereo playing full blast and Bill Haley's 'Rock Around the Clock' filled my room. At the same time I could hear Laura's feet on the floorboards as she jumped up and down to the music.

I found the noise from her room very annoying

and would complain to her at least once a week. One reply of hers was 'No one has ever complained about my music before. Perhaps when a room becomes vacant you should move downstairs.' My complaints annoyed her and most of the time she refused to turn down the volume. When we were both in of an evening the only time life ran smoothly was if we were both watching the same TV station.

I soon realized that one of Laura's favourite TV programmes was *Dallas*. I also enjoyed this series and if ever I forgot it was on I would be instantly reminded because Laura would turn up the volume of her TV set and I would hear the signature tune echoing around my room, with the result that I never missed an episode.

This state of affairs meant I could never have an early night.

I annoyed Laura further whilst we were in our kitchens. She would play her transistor radio quietly until I came along. As soon as I began to wash up she would turn the volume higher. One Saturday I opened my lower cupboard to find a saucepan and sent all the saucepans and their lids crashing to the floor. I heard a 'tut' from the other side of the partition and the radio was turned up considerably higher.

I did occasionally get into conversation with Laura after one of her quieter periods, but usually we just acknowledged each other. I did not row with her. When she knocked on my door and said, 'Don't you know it's your turn for the toilet roll?', I simply said, 'Sorry,' and put one in the holder. After this misdemeanour Sharon laughed and told me, 'Laura was complaining about you not sticking out the next toilet roll and she said, "Well, we all know when its our turn now, don't we." '

Never at any time did Laura complain about us both doing our washing on a Sunday.

Tracey and Me

Tracey and I were good friends. If we were both at home of an evening we would frequently spend the time in my room watching TV. We were usually irritated by Laura's loud TV or stereo. I would ask Tracey, 'What would you do about this?' She would shrug her shoulders and say, 'Just keep complaining.'

It was now winter and Tracey and I both smoked like chimneys. At the end of our evenings I would be forced to open my window to let the smoke out as tears would be running down my face. This would result in a smoke-free but icy room. I stored my white suitcase on top of my wardrobe and as time passed by it slowly became yellow with nicotine stains. I tried using bleach to clean it, but I was unable to remove the stains and my suitcase became too unsightly to use.

Tracey and I would sometimes go out on a Friday night to a pub with a live group and a dance floor.

One Saturday afternoon I returned to the house after having a cut and blow-dry from a local male hairdresser. Not sure if I liked my hairdo, I asked Tracey, 'What do you think of my hair?'

She looked at me and replied, 'Tell me where he is and I'll go and beat him up.'

I soon discovered trouble always followed Tracey. One week before Christmas she told me, 'I've just been made f——— redundant and my bosses can't afford to pay me any wages. Nobody got any wages today and next week it's Christmas. You should have seen the trouble in the office. One feller tried to beat up one of the directors because he didn't have any money to give his kids their Christmas dinner and nobody is likely to get a penny out of them. The entire bloody firm has gone bust. Gawd knows how I'm going to pay my rent. Everybody in the office was fuming. Now it's almost Christmas and I haven't got a f——— job. Cor, bloody 'ell.'

I sympathized. As I couldn't help her, I said, 'Sit down. I'll make you a cup of tea.'

In an effort to cheer herself up, Tracey decided to visit her aunt on the Isle of Wight for the Christmas holiday, 'to get away from it all'.

Christmas 1984

As December began I looked forward to the Christmas break, as the company I worked for closed down for ten days.

Early in December I bought presents and cards and planned my holiday. I made arrangements to spend Christmas Day with my father, to shop in the sales with a girlfriend, followed by dinner and the cinema, and to stay with my mother and aunt for a few days.

The other tenants also planned their holidays. Laura went skiing in Switzerland with a friend.

Tracey was at her aunt's. Sharon's parents were in London, living in their flat, with Sharon, her sister and brother-in-law joining them, making it a family Christmas. Peter planned to stay with his parents, eventually meeting up with Sharon and her family. This meant I was the only tenant in the house for most of the holiday.

I discovered my firm also closed at lunchtime on Christmas Eve so I phoned my friend Jessica and suggested, 'Why don't we go and see a play?'

She replied, 'That's a first-class idea. I'll look through the evening paper and give you a buzz back.'

We selected our play. She said, 'I'll book two seats and I'll meet you at Charing Cross tube at six p.m. We can have a meal first and then go to see the play.' We both made entries in our diaries.

On Christmas Eve I set off for the theatre. I waited at Charing Cross tube for one hour, with no sign of Jessica. I didn't know which theatre we were going to and I'd also forgotten the name of the play. As Jessica did not appear, I decided to have dinner in a nearby restaurant and then make my way home. I phoned Jessica as soon as I returned to the house, but there was no answer.

Christmas morning she phoned me, saying, 'I'm sorry, love, I forgot which tube I was supposed to be meeting you at. I couldn't remember whether it was

Charing Cross or the Strand. I stood at the Strand
for about forty-five minutes before I went to dinner.
Then I went to see the play since I had the tickets
and halfway through I remembered I should have
met you at Charing Cross. I'm ever so sorry, love.
Obviously I'll pay for the tickets.'

'It's all right, Jessica,' I replied. I asked, 'Did you
like the play?'

'Yes, it was terrific,' she replied.

After my ruined Christmas Eve I looked forward
to going to the sales on Boxing Day with Jessica
and to the dinner and film we were going to enjoy.

Later on Christmas morning I visited my father at
the family house. He cooked the dinner, which was
very enjoyable. We spent a pleasant day simply talking to each other and watching TV. He sympathised
with me over my disappointment the previous
evening. At eight p.m. I returned to the empty
Appleby House.

On Boxing Day I set off to meet Jessica at the local
tube. We travelled to Oxford Circus.

We looked through the sales in two major stores
and I made a few small purchases. Whilst walking
down Oxford Street I suddenly began to feel very
unwell. I slowly felt worse and worse. I was in des-
perate need of a toilet and could feel my stomach

expanding like a balloon. We managed to find a loo, which greatly relieved my predicament, but my stomach was still balloon-like and, as I was feeling dizzier and dizzier, Jessica quite rightly decided I should return home as quickly as possible. Without more ado we took the tube and, as she lived a few minutes' walk away, Jessica saw me back to my street door.

I climbed into bed and I felt really, really ill. I had violent stomach pains and every twenty minutes I had to visit the loo.

I was totally alone in the empty house.

The next day I gingerly drifted down the stairs to the telephone, clutching the banister tightly. I phoned my doctor.

He said, 'Tell me your symptoms.'

I told him.

'You have food poisoning,' he said. 'Go to the chemist and get some kaolin and morphine and that will help you,' he advised.

'What am I supposed to get?' I asked.

'Kaolin and morphine,' he repeated. Suddenly I became very dizzy. 'I'm going to faint,' I whispered down the phone.

'Put your head between your knees,' he instructed,

which I did, sinking to the stairs and just managing not to faint, but dropping the telephone receiver.

Two or three minutes later I picked up the receiver, only to hear a continuous buzz. My doctor had obviously finished our conversation. I phoned my mother and told her of my illness and that I clearly would not be able to go to Basildon as I had planned. I dragged myself up the stairs and went back to bed wondering how I was going to get to the chemist.

In the afternoon I heard the street door open and close. Realizing it was Peter, I called out to him. Fortunately he heard me and, after being told to 'Come in', he entered my room.

He looked down at me as I lay in bed and asked, 'What's the matter with you?'

I replied, 'I've got food poisoning and I'm supposed to get some medicine but I can't go out and get it and I can't remember the name of it.'

'I'll go and get it for you, Sylvia,' said Peter, asking, 'Is there anything else you want?'

'I've run out of milk,' I replied. Peter very kindly did my shopping for me. On his return he said, 'I went into the chemist and told him what you've got and he's given me this kaolin and morphine.'

'That's it,' I replied. He put the milk in the fridge

and said, 'If you want anything, just call downstairs and I'll come up and see you. I'm staying in the house overnight, but I won't be here for the next two days after that because I'm going to Sharon's parents' flat.' Peter was to stay with Sharon and her family an extra two days, making a further four days away from the house.

I was very ill. The medicine had an amazing effect and greatly improved my condition, but I was unable to eat a biscuit without violent stomach pains and an immediate journey to the loo. I made myself the occasional cup of tea, tottering from my room to my kitchen, but I had no desire to smoke or eat.

I turned on my TV to see Barry Manilow singing in a ward of a children's hospital. I lay on my bed, looking at the screen. My sense of humour left me completely and I burst into tears because it was my Christmas too and here I lay ill as well and unable to go out. I thought of all my dashed plans and sobbed.

On the sixth day I managed to get up and found it necessary to go shopping. The house was still empty. I made a short trip to the shops, willing myself not to faint, and did the shopping, buying only what was necessary. Peter returned to the house late that evening and came up to see me.

'How are you now?' he asked.

'Much better thank you' I replied.

Two days later it was time to go back to work. I was still not properly well, although considerably improved. I phoned my boss and told him of my illness. He was very sympathetic, saying, 'I'm sorry to hear this, Sylvia, and do hope you'll be better soon. Don't worry about a medical certificate and don't come back until you're properly well.'

My next call was to Basildon to my mother and aunt. Despite my condition I decided to travel down to them and thereby retrieve three days of my holiday.

On my return the house was full.

Tracey knocked on my door. She said, 'I phoned you over Christmas. Peter answered and said you were ill in bed and weren't well enough to come to the phone.'

The New Year

All the tenants returned to the house after the Christmas holiday. Laura told me what a marvellous time she'd had in Switzerland. Sharon and Peter said they'd had a pleasant time too. Tracey said her holiday was 'not too bad under the circumstances'.

I saw my doctor before returning to the office. He told me I'd had acute food poisoning and that I was now fit enough to return to work. I arrived at the office one week later than expected.

Both Sharon and Tracey were interested in my illness.

'How did you get it?' Tracey asked.

'I think it was a pork chop I bought from the butcher around the corner,' I replied.

Sharon laughed and said, 'You did it yourself, then. Pork chops have to be properly cooked.'

'Sharon,' I said, 'what I think happened is the butcher was not able to sell all his pork chops, so he put them in the freezer, then he put them out in the shop again, still didn't sell them all, so he put them in the freezer again and then back out on the counter, and then I came along and bought one. Everything I ate was properly cooked.'

Tracey said, 'Well, at least you look good.' I was half a stone lighter.

Laura used the vacuum cleaner after Sharon and, on finding it didn't work, promptly telephoned Mr Appleby to ask him to come and repair it. The following day Mr Appleby discovered it was full of twigs. He removed them and said to Laura, 'It's working properly now, but it was full of someone's Christmas tree.'

'Oh, that must be Sharon,' Laura said and continued, 'I used it after her.'

Mr Appleby went downstairs to speak to Sharon. He said, 'Another time could you be a bit more careful, please. Half your Christmas tree was in the vacuum cleaner and that's why it wasn't working.'

As Sharon was on holiday from art college she occupied herself with dressmaking and made herself a blue two-piece. She put it on to show me and boasted, 'I wore it to dinner last night round Peter's parents' house and they all admired it.'

'It looks very nice,' I said. 'And the colour suits you too.'

Sharon's two-piece simply did not fit her at all and was quite obviously a very bad attempt at dress-making.

The occupants of the house settled down to meet the New Year.

Tracey's Illness

Twelve days into the New Year I returned home from the office. I opened the street door and saw Sharon and Tracey talking outside Tracey's flat. Tracey had her sweater pulled up and Sharon was examining her stomach.

'Christ Almighty,' she said.

'What's the matter?' I asked, walking towards them. I saw Tracey's stomach. It was covered in nasty red spots. Sharon and I looked at each other and took one step back.

I said to Tracey, 'You'd better go and see a doctor.'

'I think you're right,' she said as we walked away from her.

'You don't look too good to me, Tracey,' I said.

Sharon added, 'It could be something minor, you know, perhaps an allergy.'

I returned home from work the following evening to see Sharon standing outside her kitchen talking to Tracey, who was standing in her doorway some twenty feet away.

'Did you see a doctor?' I asked Tracey.

'Yes I did and he said I've got chickenpox,' she replied.

'God,' I said, 'I've never had that. Have you, Sharon?'

Sharon didn't look too pleased and replied, 'No, I haven't either.'

We both breathed a sigh of relief when Tracey said, 'Don't worry. I don't think it's fair to give the house chickenpox so I'll go and stay with my mum until I'm better.'

When Laura returned home I told her of Tracey's predicament. She said, 'I'm sorry she's ill, but I'm glad she's going because I haven't had chickenpox either.'

On speaking to Sharon later that evening she told me, 'Peter hasn't had chickenpox.'

Tracey vacated her flat.

Two weeks passed by. As usual I returned from the office at five-thirty. Hearing the street door open and close, Tracey appeared from her flat. I was pleased to see her again and asked, 'How are you now?'

She replied, 'I'm all right, but my mother isn't. She's never had chickenpox, so when she did my washing she picked everything up with her wooden tongs, holding it as far away from her as possible, and then put it in the washing machine. She's now sterilizing the place to make sure she doesn't get it.'

'Did you itch?' I joked.

'Slightly, Sylvia. I've never scratched so much in my life,' she replied.

Tracey

After her illness Tracey tried to find herself work. Early in the New Year she had registered unemployed and received unemployment pay and housing benefit from the State. She had to borrow from her grandmother to pay her back rent and buy food as she didn't receive any wages or redundancy money from her firm.

I suggested, 'Why don't you see if the DHSS can sue them or something?'

'No, I can't be bothered,' she replied. 'I'll just have

to sort myself out another job.' She was to be out of work for the following three months.

Tracey would spend her days reading the 'Situations Vacant' columns in the newspapers and phoning up various employment agencies. As she had no money she spent most of her time in the house. She had a boyfriend she saw twice a week, I would treat her to a couple of drinks in a pub occasionally and she would sometimes spend the weekend with her gran in Dagenham, the only snag being 'I have to sleep in an armchair because there's no space.' She told me, 'I love my gran. I went to live with her when I was thirteen when my parents split up. My grandfather was alive then and my gran would let me bunk out to a disco.' Every few weeks the old lady would travel up to London to spend a day with Tracey.

Tracey lived and died in her blue jeans, possessing only one black suit, one black dress, two skirts and four sweaters, this being the only clothing she had taken when she left her husband, and now she had no money to buy herself a 'new wardrobe'. Electricity was expensive and she did not have sufficient money to heat her flat during the day. She told me, 'When I sit in my flat it's so bloody cold that when I breathe out steam goes up.'

In an effort to improve her situation Tracey's

mother made her a present of a small black and white TV set as Tracey only had her stereo for company.

Her mother upset the house by phoning at eight a.m. on two Sunday mornings to check to see if Tracey had spent the night in her flat. Fortunately Tracey had, but she had a row with her mother for telephoning so early and the calls ceased.

Returning home from work one evening, I saw Tracey sitting in Sharon's kitchen with her head in her hands.

'What's the matter?' I asked.

She replied, 'I've just found myself a temporary booking and my f——— mother has said I can't go because my gran's ill, so I've got to go down Dagenham and look after her. That's the first work I've found and it's too late to phone the agency and tell them. I'll just have to stand up their clients tomorrow.'

Sharon and I both sympathized with her.

'Why can't your mother go to Dagenham instead of you?' I asked.

'She said she'll lose her own job,' she wailed.

Tracey duly travelled to Dagenham for a few days to look after her gran.

Hearing a commotion in the hall I opened my door to experience Tracey's next disaster. Laura came out too and we heard, 'He's bloody insane,' from Tracey. I leaned over the banisters and asked, 'What's going on down there?'

Tracey replied, 'I went out with this feller twice a few weeks ago and when I packed him in he sloshed me one. Since then he's knocked on the door three times and Sharon keeps telling him I'm out, but he still turns up. Now he's knocked again and he's sitting outside waiting for me in his van. He's the size of a house and looks like a bloody gorilla. What am I going to do?' she wailed.

'Phone the police,' I said.

Sharon said, 'Oh no, we can't do that. I've just phoned Peter at work and he said the police won't come out for anything like that.'

I disagreed and said, 'If you phone them up, Sharon, and tell them it's just four women in the house and he's some type of nut, then I should think they will.'

Laura said, 'If he knocks on that door again, then I think we'd better phone the police.'

We need not have worried. Tracey's 'gorilla' sat in his van for half an hour and then drove off, and it was to be the last time he knocked.

My Male Friends

Whenever a man friend of mine knocked on the street door he came immediately under the scrutiny of both Sharon and Tracey. My first male caller was Ghalib.

Ghalib was an Iraqi who had settled in London some twenty years ago. I met him through a social club at a badminton event held on a Monday night. As Ghalib was very interested in me he made friends with me and taught me to play badminton, becoming my regular badminton partner. He was always asking me out despite my continuous, 'No thank you, Ghalib. I don't want to be more than friends.' At this time my Renault 5 car was becoming far too expensive and as the tube was only five minutes' walk away, I sold my car and didn't replace it. This meant I was unable to get to the sports centre where we played, so Ghalib very kindly volunteered to collect me and take me home in his car.

Every Monday night at quarter to eight Ghalib would knock on the street door. To begin with the door was eagerly opened by Sharon, with Tracey floating in the background. To their amusement, every time Ghalib called he would say, 'Have any lions or tigers passed through here?' this being his idea of a joke. Neither girl ever appreciated his sense of humour and on my return the first time he collected me Sharon laughed and said, 'He's an absolute wimp,' with Tracey nodding in agreement.

Sometimes, if I wasn't quite ready to leave, Ghalib would sit in my room while I combed my hair or put my handbag together. He continued to ask me out and I continued to say, 'No thank you, Ghalib.'

On my birthday I received six separate birthday cards signed 'from a secret admirer'. Each card had a drawing on it: a cake, a packet of cigarettes, a bottle of wine, a bottle of perfume, a scarf, and on the last a box of chocolates.

In the evening there was a knock on the street door. Sharon opened it and called up to me, 'It's for you, Sylvia.'

I came out of my room to see Ghalib climbing the stairs, his arms full of presents for me. He gave me a cake, 200 cigarettes, a bottle of wine, a bottle of perfume, a scarf and a box of chocolates and kissed me lightly on the lips, saying, 'Happy birthday,' and gave me a big hug.

'Are all these birthday cards from you, Ghalib?' I asked.

'Yes', he replied, adding, 'I wondered if I'd annoyed you.'

'No, of course not,' I replied and said, 'Thank you for the lovely presents, Ghalib,' thinking, 'This is very nice of you, but totally unnecessary.'

He opened the wine and poured us both a glass. Once he had drunk his he wished me happy birthday again and left the house.

One Monday night, while driving me to the sports centre, Ghalib told me his troubles. He said, 'I have just fallen in love with the most wonderful woman, Sylvia, but I am almost ill with worry because she has run away from me and I can't find her. I've tried phoning her lodgings, but she's not there any more. I feel so bad I've been to the doctor's and he's given me tranquillizers. I just cannot bear this.'

I looked at his ashen face and said, 'I'm very sorry, Ghalib. Why don't you try forgetting about her?'

'I just can't,' he replied. Our evening continued. He played badminton in a very subdued fashion.

As I was worried about him, I phoned him on the Thursday evening.

'How are you now, Ghalib?' I asked.

'Oh, I'm feeling much better, but the situation has not resolved itself. I managed to find my girlfriend, but she refuses to see me. When I spoke to her at last I told her how overwhelmed I had been with my feelings for her and she said the reason why she'd run away from me was because she'd been so over-whelmed as well and had been unable to cope with her feelings for me.'

'How are things now?' I asked.

'I'm afraid it's over, Sylvia, she just won't see me any more because it's all too much for her. But oh I remember how we hugged each other in the moon-light. It's so very sad.' he said. To a certain degree this put my nose out of joint as I had always thought Ghalib was mad about me. It was a slight shock to find he had amorous thoughts in another direction and I was no longer on his mind. Curious, I asked, 'How long did your relationship last, Ghalib?'

'It was only one date,' he replied.

My next male caller was Tony.

I met Tony through another social club. Whenever I went to a pub event Tony would frequently be there and we would spend the latter part of the evening together. Our personalities clicked and we would date occasionally, but our relationship was also spattered with rows. A few days after one of our rows Tony would phone me and ask for another date. At this particular time he'd just returned from a holiday in Spain and had phoned me.

'Hi, Sylvie. Did you miss me?' he asked.

'Not too much, Tone, I managed to cope,' I replied.

'I've brought you a present back,' he said and continued, 'did you get my card?'

'Yes, I did,' I said. I remembered the card with a topless girl in the sea and his comment on the back, 'The view is quite breathtaking.'

'Did you enjoy your holiday, Tone?' I asked.

'It was marvellous,' he replied, then suggested, 'How about the pictures tomorrow night?'

'OK,' I replied and a time was set.

Tony called to collect me. Sharon dashed to open the street door whilst Tracey hovered in the hallway.

Our evening at the cinema ended suddenly when Tony dropped me home. I said, 'I can't invite you in for a coffee Tony because it's after eleven o'clock and we're going to wake everybody up.' He was furious. A row followed, resulting in me getting out of his car and slamming the door whilst he shouted, 'You're not getting your present after this.' He sped down the road with my unseen present on his back seat. I opened the street door thinking, 'This is the last time I ever see you.'

The following evening I heard Sharon and Tracey's opinions of Tony.

Sharon said, 'I think he's a slob.'

Tracey said, 'I wouldn't go out with him, Sylvia. He looks too full of himself.'

Later during the evening Tracey noticed my long face and asked, 'What's the matter with you?'

I replied, 'I had a row with Tony and I'm waiting for him to phone so I can tell him where to go and it's annoying me.'

She said, 'Get it off your chest. Go and phone him and tell him not to bother any more.'

I took her advice and phoned Tony, saying, 'I don't want to see you again, Tony, can we call it a day please?'

He replied, 'Well, I'd already made that decision and I wasn't going to phone you anyway.'

I replaced the receiver abruptly and decided Tracey was quite right: he was 'too full of himself'.

True to his word, Tony did not phone me again.

Handicrafts

Both Sharon and Tracey admired my knitting. Sharon asked, 'Could you make me a cardigan, please?' 'All right', I replied, 'but you'll have to get the pattern and the wool.'

Hearing about this, Tracey asked me, 'Can you knit me a sweater after that?'

'OK,' I replied, adding, 'you'll have to wait for it.'

One evening Sharon knocked on my door. She gave me a very complex knitting pattern and a bagful of red wool. I set to work on her cardigan. It was so complicated it took me far longer to knit than I had anticipated. I moaned to Tracey.

'Forget about my sweater, then,' she said, which I decided to do.

Sharon had made a very unusual electric lamp at college. It had a black circular base with black wooden columns supporting a silver colander, which opened and closed to reveal an electric light bulb inside. If you preferred a dim light you simply closed the colander. If you wanted a bright light you open-ed the colander as wide as possible. The colander was made of tin with a design cut into it, making a pattern on the walls when in use. I liked it so much I said to Sharon, 'Will you make me a lamp like that while I'm knitting your cardigan?'

'Yes, of course I will,' she replied, adding, 'this one has a cream cord attached to the plug. When I make your one I'll make sure the cord is black, but it's going to take a week or so for me to do it.'

I finished Sharon's cardigan and gave it to her. She was really pleased with it.

'How's my lamp getting on, Sharon?' I queried.

'Oh, it's coming along nicely, but it's not quite finished yet,' she replied.

Two weeks later I asked about my lamp again, this time to be told, 'It's nearly finished now.'

A few evenings passed by. Sharon knocked on my door. She said, 'Here's your lamp, Sylvia. I hope you like it.'

'Thank you,' I replied. 'It looks really lovely.'

I closed the door as Sharon went down the stairs and I looked at my lamp. I thought it was beautiful, but it had a cream cord instead of the black one Sharon had promised. I told Tracey.

She said, 'That lamp is Sharon's original one. She told me she just couldn't be bothered to make another one.'

Sharon's Business Ventures

Sharon decided to leave art college as she was tired of studying and thought her various O and A levels were sufficient for any future career. There was much disagreement over the telephone from her parents, who wanted her to finish her studies, but Sharon was quite adamant, refusing to stay on and promptly left college, confident she could carve herself a stunning career as some type of executive.

Sharon attended various interviews and excitedly told me and Tracey, 'I've just found the most fantastic job. It entails three months' training, during which time I've got to conduct a survey by knocking on people's doors and finding out their views as to what type of transport they prefer, and after I've done three months of this I advance to executive level.' Both Tracey and I were delighted for her.

Two weeks later Sharon came up to me as I cooked my dinner and said, 'I've thrown my job in after all, Sylvia. It's been the most atrocious weather. I've been knocking on people's doors in the freezing cold and it's been tipping with rain and I've just had enough of it.'

'Oh, I'm sorry, Sharon' I replied and added, 'well, at least you picked up two weeks' money.'

'Oh no, I haven't,' she replied. 'I wouldn't have got paid until I'd done my three months' training and became an executive and after that they would have paid me.'

When I saw Tracey I said, 'Did you hear about Sharon's job?'

'Yes, I did,' she replied.

I said, 'She told me she didn't get paid and was supposed to work for three months and she still wouldn't have got paid.'

'Yes, I know,' she replied.

We both looked at each other in amazement.

A few days passed by. Sharon bounded up the stairs to me, saying, 'I've found myself the most marvellous job, Sylvia.'

'What is it?' I asked.

'Well, it's a top job in Harrods and I start on Monday and there's marvellous opportunities for advancement. I could work my way up the ladder.'

'What exactly is this job?' I asked.

'I'm a shop assistant on the perfume counter,' she replied.

As soon as I saw Tracey I said to her, 'Have you heard about Sharon's latest job?'

She laughed and said, 'Yes, it's a top job as a shop assistant.' Once again Sharon had surprised us.

Two Saturdays later Sharon climbed the stairs to tell me, 'I've just been sacked.'

'Why?' I asked.

'Well, I was late a few times and they didn't like it and then they wanted me to cover someone's sick leave today and unfortunately I overslept and didn't get there so they've just phoned me and told me not to bother coming in any more.' Her eyes looked at me filled with disappointment.

Sharon finally decided to return to art college.

Tracey and Bob

Tracey and Bob met each other whilst working for the same company, Bob being employed as a lorry driver. He was aged thirty, five foot eight with dark hair and of stocky build. Their friendship slowly developed into a romance during their day-to-day contact. Tracey knew Bob was married with two young children. She had also seen his wife meet him at the firm. Tracey described her as being 'very pretty, but very fat too'.

Bob's marriage broke up and it was then he asked

Tracey out and she accepted. He stayed with his wife until he found himself lodgings and gave Tracey their home telephone number, saying, 'Don't use it unless it's really important.'

Tracey soon became quite serious about him, hoping he would eventually divorce his wife, and that possibly Tracey and he might have a future together.

A few weeks into their romance their firm crashed. Bob was much luckier than Tracey; he soon found employment elsewhere.

Tracey and Bob usually saw each other twice a week. He would take her out on a Saturday night and would visit her in her flat on a Tuesday night, also filling her electricity meter when she became unemployed. Tracey told me, 'Tuesday night is our bonking night.' One Tuesday evening I saw her escorting Bob into the house and she introduced me to him. After this, whenever we ran into each other, Bob and I would stop and chat.

Tracey and I obviously had totally different tastes in men. Although Bob was pleasant to talk to, I didn't like him very much as I found him to be rather coarse.

Their relationship continued quite smoothly for a while with Bob also phoning her once a week, then suddenly Bob stopped contacting Tracey. As time progressed she became of the opinion that he must have gone back to his wife and children.

On one of our Friday night outings in the local pub Tracey told me her fears. She said, 'There's a pay phone over there next to the door. I'll give you Bob's home number and you go and phone him up to see if he's there. If he is, then he must have made it up with his wife.'

'All right,' I said, 'but what am I supposed to say?'

She thought for a minute, then suggested, 'Pretend you're canvassing for something.' She opened her handbag and took out her address book, saying, 'I'll write his number on this cigarette packet.'

Having decided what I was going to say, I walked over to the pay phone and dialled Bob's number. After a few rings a man's voice answered, 'Hello.'

I recognized Bob's voice immediately and said, 'Could I speak to the lady of the house, please?'

'The who?' replied Bob.

I found that so funny I replaced the receiver and returned to Tracey, telling her what I'd said and adding, 'That was definitely Bob on that telephone.'

Tracey looked very glum and said, 'Oh well, that's the end of that creep then, isn't it.'

A few weeks later Bob phoned Tracey at the house, but she would have no more to do with him. He rang a few times more, but Tracey would say, 'I really don't want to know. Just forget it.' He eventually stopped phoning her.

Laura's Pre-War Behaviour

All was quiet in Laura's life until Tracey moved in. Tracey proved to be a very strong character who would not take too much untoward behaviour and she was not frightened of standing up for herself.

Laura always gave the street door a hearty slam on entering or leaving the house. When there was a pile of Sharon's artwork propped up against the wall at the bottom of the stairs, Laura would make some comment to Sharon about it, one such comment being, 'I'm lucky to be able to get up these stairs, aren't I?' These remarks annoyed Sharon and she complained to me and Tracey, but said nothing to Laura.

Also Laura would stomp up the linoed stairs and would slam the door of her room behind her, and her heavy tread over the upper hallway would be clearly heard downstairs. Added to this there were times when all the occupants of the house were forced to listen to her music. All of this annoyed Sharon, but Sharon still would not comment to Laura about it.

Tracey, on the other hand, was slowly getting more and more irritated with Laura. She would complain to me, 'I always know which one of you is walking overhead. You have a very light tread, but Laura sounds like a herd of elephants clonking about and I'm fed up with that bloody music of hers. Some nights I can hear it over my TV, and what about the fuss she makes over the toilet rolls, they're only 25p each.'

Laura's loud voice on the telephone was a further source of annoyance to all downstairs.

One Sunday Tracey complained to me, 'Did you hear Laura and that friend of hers last night?'

'No. What happened?' I asked.

Tracey continued, 'Her friend stayed until two o'clock in the morning and they both woke me up as they came crashing down the stairs talking at the top of their voices and slamming the street door and they woke up Sharon and Peter too. Laura is a bloody ignorant cow.' Being a heavy sleeper, I had heard nothing.

As it was now winter, we also developed bath trouble. Sharon had explained to me when I first moved there, in the winter you did not get as much hot water for your 50p as you would in the summer. Initially all the tenants in the house were quite happy with the situation, but as the weather slowly got colder I found I was putting 50p in the bath one day, taking only half a bath, and the next day I would have cold water and would have to find another 50p for hot water. It was my opinion that my 50p a day was keeping the system working for everyone else. I tried to sort this out by telling the others what was happening and reminding them we had less hot water now that it was winter, requesting they take less for each bath. This everyone agreed to, but did not do.

I decided to stop having a bath every day, having a strip-down wash in my kitchen instead, and I wondered what would happen with the bath system once I withdrew my money.

I did not have to wait very long to find out. Sharon was the first to experience difficulties. She put 50p in the meter one day and had a bath, only to find cold water coming out of the tap the following day. This did not please her at all. She quietly went downstairs for another 50p, put the coin in the meter and had hot water again. Unable to persuade Peter to have a bath during this time, she turned the heater on again the next day and found cold water coming out of the tap once more. She was furious. She stormed out of the bathroom and stomped down the stairs, shouting to Peter, 'That f——— cow has nicked my water again.' She went into her front room, slamming the door behind her. I realized this remark was directed at Laura and Laura, who was in her room, must have overheard it, but she did nothing.

Tracey said to me, 'If Laura nicks my bath water I'll knock on her door and ask for my 25p back.'

I said, 'Supposing she doesn't give it to you?'

'I'll shake it out of her,' she replied.

And I believed her.

War broke out.

The War

Never at any time did I get involved in the War. I went about life as usual and remained on speaking terms with all four occupants, staying in my room and ignoring any disturbance outside it.

It was Peter, Sharon and Tracey versus Laura, with Tracey being the ringleader.

It began with the three occupants downstairs slamming the street door as hard as possible on entering or leaving the house and marching over the linoed hallways as loudly as possible. On entering a room they would deliberately slam the door. If they were watching Sharon's TV they would turn the volume as high as possible, leaving her door wide open. When they spoke to each other they would shout. At other times Tracey would leave her flat door open with her stereo playing full blast. When they climbed the stairs on their way to the bathroom or loo Tracey and Sharon would don stiletto heels and deliberately stomp up the stairs as loudly as possible. Peter would also stomp up the stairs instead of his usual dash.

One evening they played Tracey's stereo full blast and all three stomped over the hallway, slamming doors and shouting at each other. Laura leaned over the banister and called out, 'Can't you lot make any more noise?' There was no reply from downstairs, but the noise continued.

Laura's immediate reaction to this behaviour was to turn the volume of her stereo and TV so low that even I, living next door to her, could not hear it. I might have had a pleasant evening but for the racket downstairs and my feelings of laughter mingled with apprehension as I wondered what was going to happen next.

One Saturday afternoon Sharon and Peter were out, leaving Tracey on her own downstairs with me and Laura upstairs. This did not deter Tracey. She opened her flat door wide and turned the volume of her stereo to booming level. I was washing the dishes at the time and looked down the stairs to see Tracey mouthing to me, 'Is that loud enough?' I nodded my head vigorously. Laura remained in her room.

Tracey would still climb the stairs to see me. If she saw Laura she would give her an icy stare, which Laura ignored.

The next problem was the toilet rolls. It was Sharon's turn to put one out, but unfortunately she had forgotten. Laura knocked on her door and said, 'It's your turn to put out the toilet roll you know.'

Sharon saucily replied, 'I'm ever so sorry, I'll dash upstairs with one right away.'

Laura said, 'I think you ought to supply two toilet rolls since you've got Peter here.'

Sharon replied, 'Oh, I don't think so, Laura. Peter doesn't use one. He just does a pee and gives it a quick flick.' Laura stormed up the stairs, but Sharon did put out a toilet roll despite her sarcasm.

The problem of the bath continued with Laura being blamed, unfairly I thought, for taking other people's hot water. Sharon and Peter doubled up, Sharon having the first bath and immediately running the second for Peter. I also tried to do this with Tracey, but she liked a bath every other day, so one day I'd wash in my kitchen and share the bath with her the next day. That way we had full value for our fifty pence. I did not ask Laura how she was getting on, but I guessed she only had the one bath for her fifty pence.

One evening Laura had just entered the house and was about to unlock her door when she got into an argument with Sharon, who had just come out of the bathroom. The row ended with Sharon calling her, 'You f——— c———' as she walked down the stairs.

Laura replied, 'Would you like to come up here and say that?'

Sharon's face changed colour. She said, 'Would you like me to get Peter too?'

Laura said, 'Oh, I can't manage two of you, now can I?' whereupon Sharon ran down the remaining stairs to the safety of her room and Peter.

The War lasted three weeks.

Things came to a head one Sunday. I was washing some hand-knitted sweaters in my kitchen sink. At eleven a.m. Laura went down the stairs and out through the street door, closing it quietly behind her, to make her usual visit to the launderette. Immediately she had left the house Sharon called up the stairs, 'Sylvia, if you've got any washing to hang on the line you'd better go through now because we're locking my back door and Laura isn't going through it.'

'All right,' I replied, 'I'll be about five minutes.' I finished rinsing as quickly as possible and went through Sharon's kitchen and hung my washing on 'my' line in the back garden. As soon as I returned to the house, Sharon said, 'Right, this door is now being locked,' and promptly locked it, removing the key from the keyhole.

Approximately forty-five minutes later Laura returned with her wet washing and called out as usual, 'All right to go through, Sharon?'

I looked down the stairs to see Laura facing Peter, Sharon and Tracey.

Sharon said, 'No, I'm afraid not, Laura.'

Laura said, 'What's the matter with you? Why can't I go through?'

Sharon replied, 'Because I don't want you to.'

Laura pushed through them and strode through Sharon's kitchen and tried to open the back door, unsuccessfully.

Sharon said, 'Laura, this is my kitchen and I don't want you in it.'

Laura turned to Tracey and asked, 'Can I go through your kitchen?'

Tracey simply replied, 'No.'

Laura said, 'I'm not having this. I always go

through your kitchen to the garden, Sharon. I'm going to phone the Applebys and have them sort you out. You've both got the cheek of old nick.'

Laura picked up the receiver and dialled the Applebys' number. She said, 'Mrs Appleby, this is Laura. These two girls downstairs won't let me through their kitchens to hang my washing out. Can you sort them out, please?'

Mrs Appleby replied, 'Well, I'm sorry, dear, but there's nothing I can do. Both girls live in separate flats and no one is able to go through their kitchens without their permission. There is no right of way, dear.'

Laura yelled down the phone, 'Well this is f——— stupid, isn't it?'

She slammed the receiver back in its holder and stormed up the stairs. She hung her washing on the drying rails in the bathroom. She looked out of her half-window in her kitchen and shouted over the banisters, 'I see you let Sylvia through.' Finally she went into her room and slammed the door behind her.

The Applebys arrived at the house later that day to collect the rents. I heard the street door open and close and looked over the banisters to see Mrs Appleby. I laughed and waved at her. She shook her head in mock disbelief. She collected my rent and said, 'What a terrible state of affairs.'

Some time later I made myself a cup of tea and cut a slice of Dundee cake. As I was always watching my weight, I took the remainder of the cake downstairs with the intention of giving it to Sharon. I knocked on her door to hear, 'Come in,' from Sharon. I went into the room and was surprised to see Mr and Mrs Appleby, Tracey, Sharon and Peter obviously having some type of meeting. Sharon and Peter were sitting on the bed, Mrs Appleby was seated in the armchair with Mr Appleby and Tracey sitting on the carpet.

I said, 'I'm sorry. I didn't realize you were all in here. I wondered if Sharon and Peter would like this cake.'

'Yes, please,' said Sharon, looking at it.

Mrs Appleby said to her husband, 'There you are. Sylvia gets on with them all.' Peter kept quiet, but Sharon and Tracey told the Applebys of Laura's behaviour and her remarks about Sharon's artwork.

Mrs Appleby said, 'Laura has a nerve to complain about any mess downstairs when she has that armchair upstairs covered in old newspapers and magazines.' She said to me, 'How do you get on with Laura?'

I replied, 'Well, I don't very well, but my only real complaint is that loud stereo and TV. It's very annoying.'

Sharon said, 'One night Laura's music was so bad our light was going up and down.'

Mrs Appleby said, 'I didn't know that, dear. From now on Laura's music has to stop.'

I said, 'It's quiet at the moment. Laura isn't making a sound in that room.' I left them all in discussion and returned to my room.

The Applebys did not say anything to Laura, but they knew there was trouble in the house and this worried Mrs Appleby.

The following Sunday I heard the street door open and close and realized it was the Applebys. I stood at the top of the stairs, raised my eyes to heaven and laughed at Mrs Appleby. When she collected my rent she said, 'Sylvia, you keep me sane. I just can't stop worrying about what's happening in this house and I feel very sorry for you. You're caught in the middle of it.'

I replied, 'At least it's interesting.'

Mrs Appleby said, 'Do you know, Sylvia, when you first moved in Laura said to me, "I think you've picked a bad one there." I said, "I don't think so at all." '

After Mrs Appleby had left I began to think. Suddenly all became clear to me. I remembered how Laura had turned down the volume of her stereo at my first request and all the time I had spent trying to make friends with her and to involve her in any conversations with the others. I decided that Laura had at first thought I was trouble and had concluded that I was quite harmless. Then she reverted to her usual behaviour and up went her stereo and TV as she was no longer frightened of me. I made a mental note never to be that kind again.

The War slowly ended.

The occupants of the house settled down to a fairly quiet existence. Laura's music and TV were played very softly so I had peace in my room once more. She did not slam the street door as she used to, but she continued talking loudly on the telephone and to tread heavily up the stairs and over the upper hall-way, as was her habit.

Laura would try to get into conversation with Sharon. Sharon would reluctantly speak to her, but very politely. Laura also spoke to Peter. He would reply to her, but he still did not have much to say to either me or Laura. Tracey would give Laura icy stares and neither girl attempted any form of conversation with each other. Laura and I never really fell out so we would sometimes speak.

The bath situation did not correct itself. Sharon managed to get Peter to bath daily, thereby sharing the hot water, and I continued sharing my hot water with Tracey every other day. Laura never mentioned the bath problem to anyone.

Fortunately Laura did not ask, but the girls decided not to let her through their kitchens again and she continued to use the bathroom to dry her washing. I was let through as usual and would hang mine out every Sunday. It was at this time Laura had a small washing machine delivered and she stopped using the launderette.

On a lighter note, the bath heater began playing up. It was Sharon who discovered this. She phoned Mr Appleby and asked him to repair it. He came round the next afternoon and did so, leaving the house shortly after I came home. Around seven-thirty I decided to have a bath, but I was unable to find the plug. I went downstairs and told Tracey and Sharon. We searched the bathroom, my kitchen and Sharon's because these rooms were always left unlocked.

As we couldn't find the plug, I said, 'I think Mr Appleby must have taken it home with him.'

Sharon replied, 'Phone him up, then.'

I did so, saying, 'I think you must have taken it with you, Mr Appleby.'

He replied, 'That's very unlikely, Sylvia, but I'll have a look in my toolbox.' He returned to the phone and said, 'I'm sorry but I have got the bath plug. I'll bring it round straight away.' He arrived at the house one hour later.

By the time the bath plug had been sorted out Laura was in and she joined in what had now become a joke. This cleared the air and Laura got into conversation with Sharon. I overheard Laura say to her, 'I've just bought myself a new three-piece suite for my room. It's being delivered Saturday. Why don't you come up and see it?'

Sharon said, 'I'd love to,' but behind Laura's back, 'fancy buying a three-piece suite for this place.'

On the Saturday Tracey and I found reasons to be in the hallways as Laura's suite was being delivered. We examined it as it was carried up the stairs by two delivery men. It was the old English cottage style and looked very expensive. Once the men had left Sharon knocked on Laura's door to have a look at it. Tracey, Peter and I were not invited, so we made no comment to Laura.

I found the atmosphere peaceful, if strained, but Mrs Appleby did not like the tension in her house.

Sharon and Peter's Departure
from the House

One Tuesday in March, on a free day from college, Sharon set off to see her sister in Surrey, travelling there and back by train. On the return journey she became rather bored and decided to read her newspaper, placing her handbag on the seat beside her. When the train pulled up at her station she folded her newspaper away and went to pick up her handbag, only to find it was missing. She looked under the seat and around the carriage and accepted the fact that her handbag had been stolen. This event caused her great difficulty. Her handbag had contained her train ticket, her purse, her student card, her keys, her make-up, comb, etc.

She got off the train and explained the situation to the ticket inspector. He was not too sympathetic, but he did let her through without a ticket, whereupon she phoned up the local police station and reported the matter.

Arriving home, Sharon knocked on the street door, which was opened by Peter. She slammed the door behind her and started shouting. This attracted the attention of me, Laura and Tracey, and we all gathered round her. In a voice full of anger Sharon told us what had happened, adding, 'I just had enough money in my pocket to cover my underground fare home and although I've reported this to the police I don't think I'm ever going to see that handbag again and it had my student card with my name and address on it, with the keys to the house as well, so I'd better phone up Mr Appleby and tell him to change all the locks, otherwise we could get burgled.' Without further ado she picked up the receiver, put the 10p given to her by Peter into the slot and dialled the Applebys' number.

'Mr Appleby,' she said, 'this is Sharon. I've just had my handbag stolen and it's got my address in it and the keys to the house, so could you come down tonight and change all the locks, otherwise we could get burgled.'

Mr Appleby replied, 'I can't come down tonight, it will have to wait until the weekend.'

This was the last straw for Sharon. She yelled down the phone at him, swearing at the top of her voice, calling him all the insulting names she could think of, finally telling him, 'I'm moving out Saturday,' and slamming the phone down.

Coincidentally Saturday was also the day Sharon's lease expired and, as the situation did not alter, Sharon phoned her mother explaining her position and asked if she could move into the empty flat in west London, not mentioning Peter. As her mother agreed, Sharon arranged for the caretaker of the flats to supply her with the keys. Peter phoned a friend who owned a large van and asked him to move them on the Saturday. This being agreed, they spent their free time packing their numerous possessions into boxes and crates.

On the Friday evening I went down the stairs to see them. I asked Sharon, 'Have the Applebys been in contact with you at all?'

'No, I haven't heard a thing from them,' she replied.

'Won't you be sorry to go?' I asked.

'Not from this dump,' she replied.

I asked, 'Are you sure you're going?'

'Absolutely,' she replied.

'Well, if that's the case,' I said, 'I wonder if the Applebys will let me move down here, but I don't want to pay more than £27 a week rent.'

Sharon replied, 'Oh they'll never agree to that. They must be able to get £35 for this lot.'

I replied, 'Well, I'll see what they say, but I won't be paying that much.'

Sharon said, 'I don't think they'll agree to that, Sylvia.'

Sharon had never had keys cut for Peter as they usually spent their time together and she was always in before him of a weekday, so Tracey let Sharon into the house for their last few days.

Saturday morning Peter's friend arrived in his van and the three of them filled it with Sharon's and Peter's belongings. Sharon left a note on her kitchen table for the Applebys giving her new address, requesting them to forward her deposit there.

They said their goodbyes to everyone and closed the street door for the last time.

My Move Downstairs

The Applebys arrived on the Sunday to find Sharon's rooms unlocked and her note on the kitchen table.

Mrs Appleby came into my room to collect my rent. She said, 'What a disgraceful way for that child to behave. My poor husband, the way that child spoke to him. It was dreadful to be subjected to such abuse. And she's not given us any notice either.'

'Mrs Appleby,' I asked, 'would it be possible for me to move downstairs? The only snag is I don't know what you want for rent and I don't want to pay more than £27 a week.'

She replied, 'I'll tell my husband about it, dear, and we'll have a think, but we could get a lot of money for that accommodation.' She asked, 'Would you like to look at the rooms?'

'Yes, I would,' I replied.

Mr Appleby was in Sharon's front room. As we entered he said, 'Irene, look at this wardrobe.' Mrs Appleby and I both looked at it.

'Goodness, what a mess,' said Mrs Appleby.

Mr Appleby continued, 'God knows what Sharon thought she was doing. It looks like some attempt at revarnishing. I wouldn't mind if she'd done a good job. Now I've got to strip all this mess off and I'll have to paint it white.' He turned to me and said, 'She's not supposed to do any alterations without our permission.'

Mrs Appleby said to me, 'That was a good wardrobe before that child did this. She won't be getting much of her deposit back now. It's going to take my husband hours of work to put this right.'

Apart from the fact that it was much better accommodation, my main reason for wanting to move was to get completely away from Laura and her stereo. I did not trust her to keep things quiet.

Midweek the telephone rang. I went down the

stairs to answer it. It was Mrs Appleby. Recognizing my voice, she said, 'Hello, Sylvia, dear. Have you heard any news from Sharon?'

'No, nothing,' I replied.

She continued, 'Of course we always knew Peter was living with her, but we didn't know how long he'd been there. How long was it, dear?'

Not realizing I was being manipulated, I replied, 'Peter has always lived here. He was living here when I moved in and for some time before that.'

'Good gracious,' said Mrs Appleby. 'We didn't know that. We always had our suspicions that he was living with Sharon because when my husband came to do repairs there was always Peter's tyre marks in the snow in the front garden, but we had no idea he'd been living with Sharon for so long. And to think I deliberately gave that child such a low rent. And look how she repays me. This is absolutely disgraceful behaviour. This has really upset me.'

I said, 'I'm sorry to give you a shock, but you told me you knew their set-up.'

The Applebys came to the house the following Sunday to collect the rents as usual and to empty the meters. Mrs Appleby knocked on my door. I invited her in and she sat down in my armchair. She said, 'We've thought about your offer for downstairs, dear, and we've decided you can move down as soon as my husband has redecorated. The rent we want is £26 a week for the first year and after that it will go up to £27 a week for another year, and the only reason we are giving you such a low rent is because we trust you not to share like Sharon did. Well, does that suit you, dear?' she asked.

'Yes, it does. Thank you,' I replied. Then I asked, 'Could I have another look at downstairs?'

She replied, 'Yes, of course, dear.'

We joined Mr Appleby in Sharon's kitchen. He said, 'I'll have to completely redecorate in here, Sylvia, but the front room only needs a whitewash on the ceiling, and then I'll paint the wardrobe white and that chest of drawers. I should be finished in about a fortnight, then you can move down.'

Mrs Appleby said, 'I have some pale yellow curtains, dear, which would blend very nicely with the walls and the carpet in the front room and the armchair. Would you like them?'

'Yes, please,' I replied.

Mr Appleby said to me, 'Nearer the time, if you tell me how you want the furniture arranged, I'll sort it out for you.'

'Thank you,' I replied.

Mr Appleby decorated the downstairs flat during the daytime and would leave the house at six-thirty each evening. One evening I wanted to use the telephone. On looking at the receiver I saw a huge white handprint on it. I laughed and asked Mr Appleby, 'Did you use the phone?'

'Why?' he asked, coming out of the kitchen to look at it.

I pointed to the receiver and said, 'Your hand must have been covered in paint.'

He said, 'Oh, I'll soon get that off with some turps.'

I made my call and returned to my kitchen to cook my dinner. The house filled with the sound of Mr Appleby singing at the top of his voice: 'Ramona, I hear the mission bells above. Ramona . . .'

I eventually moved downstairs into my two rooms. Mr Appleby had made a good job of redecorating and had even washed the kitchen floor for me. I thought the front room looked a very attractive bed-sitting room. Mrs Appleby had hung the curtains in the large bay window and I liked the pastel colours and the freshness of the room.

I slowly carried my possessions down the stairs. I filled the high white shelves in the left alcove with wine and drinking glasses and some attractive orna-ments, placing my TV on a small brown wooden table underneath the bottom shelf. I made the bed with my expensive bedlinen and I was very pleased with the result.

When Tracey saw my new accommodation she said, 'I'm jealous.' Laura also viewed my two rooms and said, 'You're very lucky, aren't you?' Mrs Appleby told me, 'My husband said, "This room is the best I've seen it for years." '

Life Downstairs

One week after my move downstairs the Applebys went on holiday to Portugal. During their absence I discovered my electric cooker was not working properly. The oven took twice as long to cook a dinner and as this was becoming very expensive I decided to use the gas cooker upstairs until the Applebys returned.

Life was considerably better than living next door to Laura. Most of the time she was playing her music at a reasonable level and as we had floorboards and a ceiling between us I usually had a peaceful existence.

Returning home from the office each evening, I would sit down at my kitchen table drinking tea with the French windows opened wide. I would listen to Mo in her kitchen cooking the family dinner and talking to her children. From my front room I would hear the noises of the street and would see the passers-by through my bay window. Every Saturday night I would hear Jamaican calypso music blaring out well past midnight, but this was from a house much further down the street so it did not disturb me.

Tracey and I soon had an arrangement where we took it in turns to cook a dinner once a week. I discovered she cooked an excellent curry. If we were both home of an evening we would spend our time in my front room chatting and watching TV.

Tracey asked me, 'Are you going to let Laura through your kitchen to the back garden? Because she's not coming through mine.'

I replied, 'I don't think it's very nice if I don't, but I'm going to sort something out with her because I hate going to the launderette every week. So I'm going to do my bedlinen and bath towels in the launderette every four weeks and just handwash everything else. This means I'm going to need both washing lines once a month.'

I discussed this with Laura and said, 'You're welcome to go through as usual for three Sundays, but on the fourth Sunday I need both washing lines, so there won't be any space for you. What do you think of that?'

She replied, 'That's all right. At least it's better than using the bathroom.'

A few weeks later I answered the telephone. A woman's voice said, 'I'm Peter's mother. Do you happen to know where my son is? I find myself in the position of not hearing from my son for four weeks and I have no idea where he is.'

I replied, 'I'm sorry, but he hasn't been here at all or contacted us in any way.'

She continued, 'Do you know the pair of them have moved three times now and I don't know where they are. If he phones you, could you ask him to contact me?'

I said, 'Yes, I'll do that,' and replaced the receiver. I relayed the conversation to Tracey and we decided that Sharon must have had another row with her mother, moved out of her mother's flat, and then had rows and moved out of the next two flats.

I noticed Mo's absence from the house next door.

I could no longer hear her in her kitchen. I asked Laura, 'What's happened to Mo?'

She replied, 'She's gone on a fortnight's holiday, taking her three youngest with her, and the eldest boy is looking after the house and Bess.'

As the days passed by I noticed that although Mo's son fed and watered the dog, he would close the back door and leave her in the back garden of an evening and all weekend while he was out, and Bess would cry nonstop.

When Mo returned from holiday, I mentioned this to her. She said, 'Oh that's nice, now I can't go on holiday.'

A few weeks after my move downstairs my boss retired and I was made redundant. I found work as a temp with a local agency whilst I looked for permanent employment.

The Applebys' Return

The Applebys arrived at the house the first Sunday after their return from Portugal. They collected three weeks' rent from each tenant and emptied the meters.

When Mrs Appleby knocked on my door, I asked her, 'Did you have a good holiday?'

She replied, 'Yes, dear, and it was lovely weather and a very welcome break.' She asked, 'How have you all been getting on in the house, dear?'

I replied, 'All right. We don't hear much of Laura

downstairs and Tracey and I are friends so things are quite peaceful at the moment.'

She said, 'Oh, I am glad, dear. I don't like trouble in my house.'

As we were nearing summertime, even the bath situation resolved itself, with no problems between the three of us.

Tracey and Laura still did not speak to each other, but Laura and I would have brief conversations.

I told Mrs Appleby about the oven. 'It takes twice as long as it should to cook anything so I've been using my "old" gas cooker upstairs. I think you need to replace Sharon's one. Is it possible to swap it over with my gas one because that was perfect?'

Mrs Appleby replied, 'I'll have to ask my husband, but we do know this one is on the faulty side, but perhaps we can have it repaired. Until then I should continue using the gas one upstairs. Is everything else all right, dear?'

I replied, 'Yes, everything's fine. I much prefer living downstairs, at least I have a view.'

The Applebys had an engineer inspect my oven. Mr Appleby told me, 'The engineer says it's beyond repair, so I'll have a look at some reconditioned cookers for you. We can't change over with the one upstairs because we haven't got gas supplied in your kitchen.'

Tracey's Latest Beau

Tracey and I had planned to go to a wine bar one Saturday night. As evening approached, I had a bath, washed my hair, saw to my make-up and donned my freshly pressed black cords and hand-knitted mauve jumper, and waited for Tracey to return from a day spent visiting her mother. She did not get on with her mother at all and she returned to the house in a bad mood. She said, 'I don't think Saturday night is a night for wine bars so I'm not going. I think I'll go and see my gran.'

'Thanks, Tracey,' I replied.

She left the house, leaving me with an empty evening and dressed for a night on the town. I turned on my TV and electric fire and lay on my bed watching the various programmes. Around eleven o'clock I realized my eyes were closing. Suddenly it was five o'clock in the morning, my room was baking hot and my TV was hissing. I switched off both appliances and opened a window. As I was fully dressed I washed my face, cleaned my teeth, combed my hair and didn't bother with any further toilet until the following morning.

I forgave Tracey her misdemeanour. The following Saturday we set off for a night of dancing in London's West End. We travelled there by tube. Inside the disco we sat at a table overlooking the dance floor and bought our drinks. I noticed we had the attention of two men, both dressed smartly in dark suits. I was quite interested in the younger one. I decided he was aged thirty-eight. The other man appeared to be in his mid-fifties and well past my age limit. The older man asked Tracey to dance. Whilst she was dancing I noticed the younger man looking at me. Tracey's partner eventually returned her to our table and rejoined his friend. Tracey told me, 'They're two Yanks on holiday over here. I don't fancy the older one, but the other one's really tasty.'

A few minutes later the older man walked over to our table and asked me, 'Can me and my friend join you two?'

As neither Tracey nor I were interested in him, I politely replied, 'I'm sorry, no thank you.' He returned to his friend.

Tracey moaned. 'What did you do that for? We could have had a dinner out of them.'

I replied, 'Yes, but you didn't like your one.'

She said, 'I could have ditched him later, but you liked your one. Don't ever do that again,' she ordered. Some minutes later we saw our Yanks leaving the dance hall.

We both had several dancing partners. I didn't find anyone I considered suitable to date, but Tracey returned to our table with a very attractive dark-haired man aged about thirty-four. As the disco was very loud I didn't have much conversation with him, but I thought he was an acceptable beau.

Towards the end of the evening Tracey and I had to decide whether we should leave immediately to catch the tube or hire a taxi to take us three-quarters of the way home then walk the remaining distance in the early hours, as a taxi to our door would have been over our spending limit.

Her partner said, 'You two girls had better go home by tube. There are some very funny people walking about out there at this time of night. You could run into trouble.'

Tracey was undeterred, but it would have been a very long walk home and I decided he was right.

'We'll catch the tube, Tracey,' I said standing up. She grimaced, but said, 'Goodnight,' to her partner and quietly followed me.

On the journey home Tracey told me all about her date. 'His name is Ali and he's from Egypt,' she said, adding, 'he's been over here for about ten years and he owns a delicatessen in Wimbledon, plus he's got his own house and he owns a couple of flats and lets them out. He's going to phone me Monday. I think he's lovely. What do you think?'

I replied, 'Well, I couldn't hear much of what he said, but he seemed all right to me.'

We arrived home safely, having just caught the last tube.

Tracey was out of work at this time and still had few clothes.

Ali phoned her on the Monday night and they arranged a date for the Tuesday evening, with Tracey travelling to his delicatessen, where he was going to cook her dinner.

I saw her on the Wednesday evening and asked, 'How did you get on last night?'

She replied, 'I got to his deli and he cooked me the

most marvellous dinner. Then we went back to his house and I stayed the night.'

'Did you sleep with him?' I asked.

'Yes,' she replied, 'but nothing happened. In the morning he gave me a tenner to cover my fares.'

Tracey and Ali's relationship lasted four months. To begin with she would see him most weekends and two evenings in the week, sleeping overnight with him. As she had few clothes and no money to buy more, she soon exhausted her wardrobe. Feeling sorry for her, I offered, 'Why don't you have a look through my wardrobe and see what you would like to borrow.'

Tracey was delighted and inspected my clothing, choosing my new lilac two-piece. I said, 'I'm sorry, but I've only worn that twice. You'd better choose something else.'

She finally selected a black and white cotton two-piece, a pink lurex dress and two sweaters. She wore the two-piece on her next date with Ali and told me he'd said, 'I really like that outfit, it looks good on you.' As time went by Tracey wore the two-piece on a few more dates. Each time Ali made the same comment.

Tracey said, 'Ali is so good to me. He says, "You haven't got any money, have you?" And when I say, "Yes, I have," he says, "Show me," and since I can't he opens my handbag and puts a tenner in it. He knows I haven't got many clothes so he takes me to a Sunday market and so far he's bought me a denim jacket, a weekend bag and six lovely dresses which I've left in his wardrobe. He keeps telling me how much he loves me and he wants me to get engaged. So I might just do that.'

I was very pleased for her and said, 'Lucky you, Tracey. I hope things work out all right.'

As Tracey spent so much of her time with Ali in Wimbledon I didn't see very much of her and our weekly dinners and evenings out ceased. I also had to rely on my alarm clock to wake me in the mornings, which was rather hazardous.

Tracey's Departure

Tracey eventually found herself a job as a telex operator in the City. This coincided with her mother asking her to return home. Tracey said, 'My mum said I wouldn't have to pay any rent and it's a proper home, not like this dump. I'd only have to pay for my food. The train goes straight through to the City. So I think I'll give it a try.'

I said, 'Tracey, you don't get on with your mother, do you? It's a bit silly going to live with her again, even if it's a lovely home, because you're just going to have a lot of rows and you'll have to move out, won't you?'

Tracey replied, 'I get on with her all right at the moment and she is my mother, so I'm moving in with her. But I'll come round to you once a week and we can do our dinners again.'

I asked, 'So when are you going then?'

She replied, 'I think I'll go this weekend, but don't tell the Applebys because I owe them some rent and I'm going to do a bunk.'

I said, 'Bloody hell, Tracey! Poor Mrs Appleby! And I'm going to be stuck with Laura!'

Tracey said, 'Well, you talk to Laura sometimes, don't you?'

Tracey packed her suitcases on the Friday night and left Appleby House with her few possessions mid-morning on the Saturday, travelling by minicab to her mother's home.

Hearing Tracey going backwards and forwards with her clothing, stereo and TV, Laura came out of her room into the upper hallway. She looked over the banisters and quietly watched Tracey vacate the premises. As she finally went out the street door, Tracey said to me, 'I'll give you a ring and let you know when I'll be coming round. Bye.'

I replied, 'All right, 'bye'. She closed the street door behind her.

Laura asked me, 'Has she moved out?'

I replied, 'Yes.'

We both stared at each other.

Laura finally said, 'Blimey, this is a right house to live in, isn't it.'

Tracey's departure left me in an unpleasant position. I didn't know whether to phone Mrs Appleby and tell her Tracey had left or to leave her to find out when she came to the house the following day. I chose the latter course.

The Applebys arrived on the Sunday as usual. I called Mrs Appleby into my front room and said to her, 'I'm sorry, but Tracey moved out yesterday.'

Mrs Appleby gave me a look of horror and said, 'She's moved out!'

'Yes,' I replied.

She went into the hall and said to Mr Appleby, 'Sylvia's just told me Tracey moved out yesterday.'

Mr Appleby replied, 'What, with no notice? And she owes us some back rent, doesn't she?'

The Applebys let themselves into Tracey's empty flat and found her keys on the kitchen table.

I watched them from the hallway. As Mrs Appleby passed me she said, 'I've really had enough of this bad behaviour. That girl owes me money.' They collected Laura's rent and left the house.

Tracey phoned one evening in the week and asked, 'What did the Applebys say?'

I replied, 'They weren't very pleased at all, but they didn't say much except you owe them some rent.'

She replied, 'Well, they still have my deposit, so that will have to do them.' She asked, 'How are you getting on with Laura?'

I replied, 'All right, I suppose. We don't see very much of each other.' I asked her, 'When are you coming round?'

She said, 'Not this week because I'm too busy seeing Ali and working. I'll phone you next week.'

'OK,' I said, 'I'll hope to see you some time next week then.'

The following Sunday the Applebys came to the house once more. Mrs Appleby knocked on my door. She said, 'Could I come in, dear?'

'Yes,' I replied, opening the door wider.

She sat down on my yellow armchair and said, 'I'm sorry, dear, but Mr Appleby and I have decided to close the house down. Quite frankly I just cannot take any more bad behaviour from this house. When I was on holiday I couldn't stop worrying about the goings on here and my holiday was completely ruined. Now we have Tracey moving out like this. I'm afraid I cannot take any more, so we have decided to give you and Laura two months' notice to find lodgings elsewhere and, as we promised you you could stay here for two years, dear, we think it's only fair that we pay your agency fee for your next accommodation, and Mr Appleby will move you himself. I'm sorry to disappoint you, dear, but I just can't stop worrying about the happenings in this house. We've also decided to sell it. We're going to have it converted into two flats and put them up for sale. I'm very sorry about this, dear, but two months does give you plenty of time to sort out something suitable.'

I had sat in silence listening to Mrs Appleby. Finally I said, 'Well, I do see your point of view. This house has been a disaster ever since I've been here. It's a great pity to have to move since I've settled so nicely, but it's very kind of you to pay my next agency fee.'

Mrs Appleby said, 'We're not going to do the same for Laura. She will just get two months' notice.' She continued, 'We have arranged to have Tracey's gas meter cut off, so we'll be in during the week to see that goes through all right.'

I said, 'Tracey didn't have any money, so I think you're going to find she owes the gas man quite a bit.'

Mrs Appleby replied, 'Well, we'll find out about it

in the week. We have also arranged to have all the meters cut off at the end of August and by then you and Laura should have found yourselves something.'

I said, 'I'll be sad to go, but both of you have been very good landlords to everyone.'

Mrs Appleby said, 'Thank you, dear.' She rose from the chair saying, 'Now I'll have to tell Laura.'

After the Applebys had left the house, Laura and I spoke to each other in the hallway.

She said, 'This is bloody all right, isn't it? I've been here five years and because that silly cow does a moonlight flit she's got both of us into trouble and we've got to move too.'

'Yes, I know,' I replied and asked, 'what are you going to do?'

She said, 'I think I'll go home to my parents in Harlow for a while. I suppose I might be able to buy my own flat there. My three-piece suite will have to be squashed into my parents' house. Until I had all that trouble I always liked living here. So what are you going to do?'

I replied, 'I'll just find myself another room locally. It's a pity to leave since I've got such nice accommodation. I really like my front room and I love sitting in my kitchen with the French windows open.'

Tracey telephoned in the evening. I told her the results of her early departure. She said, 'I'm really sorry. It didn't occur to me the Applebys would close the house.'

Mrs Appleby collected my rent the following Sunday and said, 'You were right about Tracey's gas meter, dear. We had to pay the man £4 26p.'

Life with Laura

Laura and I were on fairly sociable terms. I didn't particularly like her, but we had to live in the same house. I didn't forgive her for the inconsiderate way she had behaved when I had lived next door to her, but she did have her good points and I thought she didn't fully understand the effects of her bad behaviour.

After Tracey left the house, Laura would pay me visits in my room. Several times she tried to make a friend of me. During one of our conversations I mentioned a Sunday market. Laura said, 'Camden Town has a good market on a Sunday morning. If ever you want to go there I'll come with you.' She made one or two further suggestions for us to go out together, but I always sidestepped them.

Laura still slammed the street door and clattered up the stairs, but I realized this was simply a habit of hers, with no offence meant in any way.

We did have a minor set-to one weekend. Although her music was usually considerably quieter than it had been, one Saturday morning I was woken at nine-thirty by her blaring stereo. This really annoyed me. Also, around ten a.m., she vacuumed her room, all of this being directly overhead. I didn't say anything to her, but I made a mental note to do precisely the same to her the following Saturday, which I did. I don't think Laura quite realized why I was so noisy, but she certainly noticed. She didn't speak to me at all over the weekend. Knowing I had a day's holiday on the Monday, when she set off for work she crashed the street door shut and spent several minutes lifting one of the metal dustbin lids up and down in the front garden. Fortunately I had woken very early, but I remembered something Sharon had said about Laura. 'I know how nasty she can be.'

We had another set-to over the washing lines in the back garden. I had let Laura through my kitchen to hang out her washing on three consecutive Sundays as we had agreed and the Saturday before the fourth Sunday I reminded Laura, 'Don't forget I have both washing lines all to myself tomorrow.'

She replied, 'OK'.

On the Sunday I took two full laundry bags to the launderette and came back to the house and hung my washing on the lines. One hour later Laura came down the stairs, saying, 'All right to go through, Sylvia?'

I said, 'Laura, we have an agreement that I have the washing lines to myself once a month. There just isn't any space for you.'

She said, 'Well, it's only a few bits and pieces. I really don't think I'm going to bother you to that degree.'

I replied, 'Well, I'm sorry, but both lines are full up and if this is how you're going to behave, then how about you don't go through my kitchen at all.'

Laura said, 'Oh, thanks very much,' and stormed up the stairs.

On the Monday evening I turned the tap on to have my second bath, only to find cold water coming out instead of hot. I realized that Laura had deliberately taken my bath water. I went downstairs and found another 50p coin. I also noticed that Laura, who had previously shouted over the banisters to Peter for not cleaning the bath, had now taken up his bad habit. Each time I ran a bath I found it was rinsed but not cleaned, usually with a tidemark around it. I said nothing to Laura. I cleaned the bath before I got in it and only gave it a quick rinse after I'd used it. That way we both faced a dirty bath.

Laura didn't ask to go through my kitchen again and we stopped speaking to each other.

Tracey's Latest Beau
Continued

Tracey would visit me every week and we would take it in turns to cook dinner. She told me, 'I like my job and now I've got some money to spend for a change.'

'How is life with your mother?' I asked.

'Oh, all right. She doesn't bother me and lets me do what I want,' she replied.

'How are you getting on with Ali?' I asked.

She replied, 'We keep having rows and I don't

know whether I'm still going to get engaged to him. He's very possessive.'

I didn't question her further, but on her second visit she said, 'I think I'm going off Ali, you know.'

'Why?' I asked.

She replied, 'I just don't like him any more.'

On her third visit she said, 'I didn't like to tell you before because I thought you'd tell me off, but I'm sick and tired of Ali.'

I asked, 'Why?'

Tracey laughed and said, 'You know he's got tight curly hair?'

I said, 'Yes.'

She giggled and said, 'When he goes to bed he wears a hairnet to make sure his curls don't move in the night.'

We both laughed. She paused and said, 'I'm really really sick of him. He never comes over to me and Wimbledon is a long way to go after work. When I get there some nights I have to work in the deli because he serves meals there. On a Friday night I have to go straight to his house to cook his dinner and then I'm expected to do the housework.'

I interrupted, 'Have you got the keys to his house?'

'Yes,' she replied and continued, 'all right, he gives me money for helping him and all that, but I'm fed up. I'm working these days and I don't want to do any more of an evening.'

I said, 'Well, couldn't you straighten him out?'

She replied, 'I don't think so. Anyway he's a bit funny.'

I asked, 'What do you mean?'

She replied, 'He keeps taking me up wrong. When I first went out with him I would say something and he would think I was being funny and he'd lose his temper and walk out of the room to calm down. Then one night he invited two friends round and I cooked dinner for the four of us. I served the dinner and Ali thought I'd said the wrong thing again, so he smashed a wine glass on the table and the glass went into everyone's dinner so I had to throw it all away. Then the other night I said something else he didn't like, so he punched me in the face.'

'Do what!' I said. 'You must be joking. You don't go out with someone who punches you in the face, Tracey.'

She said, 'I did punch him back.'

I said, 'You can't have a feller that's violent. Get rid of him. If you marry him he'll probably get worse and what's he going to be like with the children? He'll probably get violent with them too. What else has he been doing?'

She replied, 'Nowadays instead of walking out the

room when I annoy him, he shoves me. And he's got a criminal record.'

I asked 'What for?'

She replied, 'GBH. And he's been told that the next time he appears in court he'll go to prison.'

I said, 'Bloody hell, Tracey. You pick up all the wrong fellers.'

'Well, you said you liked him,' she argued.

I replied, 'Yes, I did, but I only saw him for about twenty minutes and then I couldn't hear what he was saying.'

Tracey said, 'Oh, another thing. He's been married. He married a sixteen-year-old girl a couple of years ago and now they're separated.'

I said, 'What's a man of his age doing with a young girl of sixteen? I don't like him at all, Tracey. My honest opinion is get rid of him.'

Tracey said, 'We did have a row in the week and we parted, but he phoned me up again. As I was going to marry him and I did love him, I said I'd go round there Saturday.'

'Don't you dare, Tracey. Get rid of him, he's trouble,' I ordered.

She replied, 'Well, I did love him, Sylv.'

I said,' Tracey, just get rid of him. You must be nuts to fall for a man like that.'

Tracey thought for a while and said, 'Oh, all right.

I suppose you're right. I could finish up with no teeth, couldn't I?' She paused and continued, 'You know, I never had full sex with him. Although we always slept together, I said I didn't want to and he always said he'd wait until I was ready. He's not all bad, is he?'

We were silent for a while. Then Tracey said, 'I won't go there Saturday, but half my clothes are in his wardrobe and I want those lovely dresses he bought me.'

Tracey phoned me the following Sunday from her mother's. She said, 'I finished with Ali. I phoned him up yesterday and said I'd changed my mind and that it's best not to see him again.'

I said, 'Good for you, Tracey. How did he take it?'

She replied, 'He was upset about it and he said he loved me. Then I said, "I'll come round to pick up my dresses," and he said if I didn't want him I couldn't have my dresses back. He didn't buy all of them. There's a lot there that I bought, so I told him that and he said I couldn't have them unless I had him too.'

Tracey came to see me on the Wednesday night. She said, 'I think I'll go round Ali's when he's working in the deli and nick my dresses out of his wardrobe.'

I said, 'It'll be a scream if he's hiding in the wardrobe and sticks out his arm and grabs you.'

'Oh, don't,' she gasped. She thought for a while and said, 'I suppose the best idea is just to let him keep them in case he catches me. Then I'll be for it, but I think I'll phone him again and have one last try to see if I can get those dresses back.'

She went into the hall and used the phone, returning a few minutes later. She told me, 'He said he's taking all my stuff out of his wardrobe and he's going to keep everything in the deli so I can't have anything back unless I see him again. So I said, "Balls to you," and put the phone down on him.'

I said, 'That puts paid to that, then, doesn't it?'

A week or so later Laura and I were alone in the house one Thursday night. At nine p.m. the telephone rang. As I lived downstairs, answering the phone was my job. I lifted the receiver and said, 'Hello.' A man with a foreign accent said, 'I want to speak to the woman who lives upstairs.'

I said, 'Just a minute,' and called out, 'Laura. There's a call for you.'

'Who is it?' she asked as she came down the stairs.

'I don't know,' I replied.

She took the receiver and said, 'Hello . . . Yes that's right. . . . Oh no, that's not me, you want the other lady who lived upstairs. She's moved to downstairs front now and you were just speaking to her.' She passed the phone to me.

I asked her, 'Who is it?'

She said, 'I don't know.'

I spoke into the mouthpiece and asked, 'Who is it, please?'

The man replied, 'I'm Ali.'

I said, 'What do you want?'

He said, 'I'm going to come over there and f——— duff you over. You took my Tracey away from me. You stopped her from seeing me and I'm going to f——— duff you over. You should mind your own f——— business.'

Shocked, but keeping calm, I replied, 'We do have a police force, you know.'

He said, 'I don't give a f— for the f——— police. No one f— me up and I'm going to f——— kill you.'

I put the phone down, completely astounded. Laura was standing on the stairs beside me, so I told her it was Tracey's ex-boyfriend and repeated the entire conversation.

She said, 'Blimey, there's only the two of us here.'

I said, 'You want to be careful, Laura, because we look alike and he only saw me once.'

She marched past me and said, 'We'd better bolt this street door,' and did so.

By now I was feeling slightly better and said, 'Well, this is nice, isn't it.'

Laura laughed and said, 'If I hear a noise I'll come down and see how you are.'

I said, 'He knows I'm downstairs front now.'

I returned to my room and thought about the situation as I selected my clothes for work in the morning. I hung my skirt and top on the wardrobe handle and put my bra and briefs on my armchair.

An hour later I called up to Laura, 'I'm going to report Ali to the police. He owns a delicatessen and I know the name of it and where it is, plus I know his full name, so they ought to be able to trace him. There's no way I'm sitting here waiting for him to come and duff me over.'

Laura laughed and said, 'I think that's a good idea.'

I picked up the telephone receiver and eventually spoke to the local police station. I was told two police-men would be coming to see me later in the even-ing. Laura had been listening to the call. She said, 'This is a joke, isn't it?'

At eleven p.m. a police car parked outside the house and two policemen strode up our pathway. Laura had been looking out of her window. She raced down the stairs. I opened the street door and all four of us went into my front room. Laura and I were in our dressing gowns ready for bed and by now I saw the funny side of the situation. They were two very young policemen aged about twenty years old. I said to them, 'Please sit down.' As there was only the one armchair, Laura and I remained standing. One policeman sat on the bed and the other one went to sit on my armchair. Both Laura and I noticed my bra and briefs. We giggled as he sat on them.

The policeman sitting on my underwear asked several questions and made various notes on his notepad. He said, 'This matter will be taken very seriously. Threatening to kill someone is a very serious offence.' I offered them a cup of tea, which they refused. As they left the house, one of them said, 'We'll be getting in touch with you.'

Laura bolted the street door once more. We bade each other goodnight and returned to our rooms. I collected my used coffee cup and put it in the kitchen sink. I had been sewing buttons on earlier in the evening. As I picked up my heavy glass button jar to put it away it slipped from my grasp and made a resounding thud on the carpet. Hearing this, Laura called down the stairs, 'Are you all right, Sylvia?'

I walked into the hallway and said, 'I dropped my button jar.'

She said, 'Well, goodnight again. I hope you get to sleep.'

I turned my light off and went to bed, but I didn't get to sleep. I lay there thinking over the events of the evening. I was still awake at one a.m. My ears pricked up as I heard slow, deliberate footsteps coming up the road. They stopped immediately outside our house. This worried me, so I got out of bed and gently opened a slit in the closed curtains so that I could see out without being seen. The slow footsteps started up again and I saw very clearly who it was. It was a uniformed policeman, who I assumed had given the house a security check just in case. Feeling reassured, I climbed back into bed and this time I went to sleep.

In the morning I dressed for my local temporary booking. Laura was first out of the house. As she passed my door she called out, 'Are you all right in there, Sylvia?'

I replied, 'Yes, thanks.'

By this time the situation amused both of us, but when it was my turn to leave the house my nerve began to go. I carefully locked my two rooms. I opened the street door at great speed and slammed it behind me just in case Ali was on the doorstep waiting to push me back into the empty house. Once in the street I saw other people making their way to work. I hurried through our back turnings to the main road. As I turned our corner, I suddenly realized, 'God, I'm wearing that cotton two-piece Ali liked so much. Oh shit.' Once on the main road I relaxed totally because it was a busy street full of people and cars journeying to work.

At my temporary booking I forgot the incident until it was time to return home. As I alighted from the bus once again my nerves began to shake. I warily entered our back turnings, looking to see whether there were any foreign gentlemen about who resembled Ali. I knew Laura would not be home until about six-thirty and as it was only five-twenty I cautiously entered the house. Before I put the key in the street-door lock I looked behind me. On seeing the pathway was clear I hurried in swiftly, closing the door. I worried in case Ali was already in the house and quickly unlocked my kitchen, closed the door and relocked it, and opened my French windows to hear the reassuring sounds of Mo and her children in their kitchen. I sat at the table drinking tea until I heard Laura come in.

I called out, 'Is that you?'

She laughed and replied, 'Yes, you're quite safe.'

As Laura was in, I relaxed and went about the house in a normal manner.

Later in the evening Tracey phoned. I told her all that had happened and she burst into tears. 'I'm sorry

Sylvia. I wish I'd never met him,' she said and added, 'he's got two cars. One's white and the other one is red.'

I spent the Saturday shopping and cleaning my rooms. On the Sunday I walked through the back streets to visit my father. Before leaving the house each time I looked through my bay window to see if there were any white or red cars parked outside.

Late Sunday evening the telephone rang. A man's voice asked, 'Could I speak to Miss Smith, please?'

I replied, 'Speaking.'

The man continued, 'This is DC Pointer from the local CID. We've been sorting out your little matter and you won't be getting any more threatening calls because we are monitoring your number.'

I asked, 'Have you seen Ali?'

He replied, 'No.'

I asked, 'When you do, can you get my friend's dresses out of his deli because he won't give them back to her?'

He replied, 'Nice try, but we won't be going to see him. We don't think it's fair to see him in his shop in front of his customers, but what we're going to do is phone him up and frighten him. So you won't be seeing him again.'

I told him what Ali had said about the police force.

He replied, 'That's what he said, is it? Don't you worry, we'll soon sort him out. I think you can now forget all about the matter.'

I repeated the conversation to Laura. She laughed.

Although I was very relieved by DC Pointer's call, I still felt nervous when I was alone in the house.

The telephone rang again and this time it was Tracey. I told her the recent events. She said, 'Thank God that's sorted out, but I'm never going to get those dresses back now.'

The Closedown

I took advantage of my two months' notice and didn't look at other properties until one month had elapsed. Finally I found an excellent bedsit a few streets away.

I told Mrs Appleby my news when she came to collect the rents. She said, 'Tell the accommodation agency to send your bill to me, dear, and let me know when you want my husband to move you.'

I said, 'This is very nice of you, Mrs Appleby.'

She said, 'Would you like anything from the house,

dear? I've promised a friend she can have the vacuum cleaner, but we don't want any of the furniture, so if there's anything at all you would like just take it with you.'

I said, 'This is terrific of you! Do you mean I can take a wardrobe if I want to?'

She replied, 'Yes, dear, anything at all, but I'm not going to do the same for Laura. I don't think she's behaved herself very well in my house and in the past she's been very rude to me.'

Buying my own flat was a dream of mine. With this in mind I thought about the contents of the house and phoned my father to ask him if I could store a few things in my old bedroom. As he said I could, I made out my list. I selected my electric fire, Sharon's fairly new fridge, my excellent gas cooker from upstairs, my white bedside chest of drawers, some cups, saucers, pots and pans, and my orange and cream waste bins. When I saw Mrs Appleby again, I told her what I'd chosen and asked if that was all right.

She replied, 'Yes, of course, dear. We have no use for them, but where are you going to put them?'

I replied, 'In my old bedroom at home.'

She said, 'I'll ask Mr Appleby to deliver them for you.'

I said, 'I'd like to move on the twenty-fourth.

Could Mr Appleby take the furniture to my father's house first and then move me into my bedsit after that?'

She replied, 'I'm sure that can be arranged, dear. You've been a very good tenant and we do appreciate you leaving the house within the time we specified. It's a pity I can't say the same about Laura. She says she can't move out until a week after her two months' notice runs out.'

I told Laura the date I was moving. On my last day she said to me, 'I know we haven't always seen eye to eye, but I wish you luck.'

The Applebys arrived on the twenty-fourth as arranged. Mr Appleby hauled my furniture items unaided into his station wagon.

Laura saw the fridge going through the street door and asked, 'What's this?'

I replied, 'Mrs Appleby said I could take a few things.'

At my direction Mr Appleby drove through the back streets of the town to my father's house. As my father was too old to help him, he struggled up the stairs single-handed, depositing all the furniture in my old bedroom.

We returned to Appleby House and filled his station wagon with the belongings to be taken to my bedsit. Our task completed, I called from the bottom of the stairs to Laura, 'Goodbye, then.'

She walked into the upper hallway and replied, 'Good luck.'

I kissed Mrs Appleby goodbye in the gateway of the house and sat down in Mr Appleby's station wagon. As he drove me to my next accommodation Mrs Appleby remained in the gateway, waving until we were out of sight.

The End

WOODY ALLEN

Complete Prose

PICADOR   £7.99

Although Woody Allen is best known for his cult movies, he is also a writer of outstanding wit and skill. Dip into this collection of fifty-two pieces for hilarity, deadpan weirdness, and some extremely outlandish ideas.

Do you want to hear about the time Hitler went for a haircut? Or why Woody reveres Socrates? Have you ever wondered what would have happened if the Impressionists had actually been dentists? You can learn much about history – the piece on the invention of sandwiches is eye-opening – or modern life in this laugh-out-loud collection of thoughts, observations, diaries and stories from one of the most original minds and wonderfully comic voices of our time.

Woody Allen was born in New York in 1935. He began his career writing comedy and doing stand-up, but soon graduated to film, making his name with such contemporary classics as *Annie Hall*, *Manhattan*, *Hannah and her Sisters* and *Husbands and Wives*. His distinctive perspective and brand of humour have made him a household name. He lives in New York.

'It's no secret that Allen's short stories are just as entertaining and accomplished as his films . . . Allen's witty stories satirize contemporary society and classic modern literature in a style that is characteristically breathless, off the cuff and brilliant'
Observer

ANTHONY McCARTEN

The English Harem

PICADOR £7.99

Tracy Pringle is a supermarket checkout girl with a lively imagination. In her mind her customers are not bored and tired Londoners with screaming children, but the likes of Princess Leia and Omar Sharif. It's not surprising she turns a blind eye when Queen Elizabeth I pops a packet of Bakewell Tarts into her handbag without paying, but unfortunately the management don't see it that way, and Tracy is forced to find herself another job.

But nothing can prepare her for the new life that lies in wait at the Taste of Persia restaurant, where our heroine falls headlong into dinner plates, Islam, and a rather tricky domestic arrangement . . .

'A sparkling, fantastical tale'
Eve

'McCarten's novel hovers between indignant satire and engaging comedy of manners while sounding a clarion call against the bigotry and intolerance in our society'
Sunday Times

'Anthony McCarten's sparkling new novel manages to deal with big issues – cultural differences, religion, marriage – in a funny and often very moving way'
Dublin Sunday Tribune